Love
FOR ALL
SEASONS

Love
FOR ALL
SEASONS

EIGHT
WAYS TO
NURTURE
INTIMACY

JOHN TRENT, Ph.D.

MOODY PRESS

CHICAGO

ISBN: 0-8024-4183-1

1 3 5 7 9 10 8 6 4 2

Printed in the United States of America

To my wife, Cindy,
a loving and faithful traveling companion
through the springs and summers of our lives.
As the seasons unfold in the years to come,
I thank God that you are my friend,
lover, and life-partner.

STEPPING INTO SPRINGTIME

Welcome to a journey toward intimacy, a journey that can lead you to a love for all seasons. You have picked up a book that I believe can make a major, positive impact on your marriage or courtship. That's because it looks at eight ways to nurture intimacy contained in the greatest of all earthly love stories, the Song of Songs. It's the story of two best friends and lovers, overflowing with passion and promise.

The story of Solomon and his bride can help us learn about a love that can endure in our lives. Their story is also a marriage manual that can guide husbands and wives in the wise ways of love.

Solomon puts his principles in picture form, and we'll look at eight that comprise a gallery of loving thoughts, attitudes, and actions for married couples and those looking toward marriage. (In an earlier booklet, *Eight Steps to Intimacy*, I outlined eight pictures specifically drawn for men.) While we'll gain wise counsel on physical intimacy, intimacy between a man and a woman includes much more. The eight principles for a lasting love will include specific ways to enhance understanding and deepen the emotional and spiritual bonds between the two of you. We'll also see how closeness can be gained in character, communication, and everyday caring acts as well.

It's my prayer that your look at these nurturing ways of love will cause your relationship to become as fresh and refreshing as spring and that you too will find a love for all seasons.

John Trent, Ph.D.
Phoenix, Arizona

CONTENTS

ACKNOWLEDGMENTS

I gratefully acknowledge the team of new friends at Moody Press who helped give birth to this book, especially Jim Bell, Jim Vincent, and Greg Thornton.

Thanks too for my Encouraging Words staff and Board of Directors. The staff team closed ranks while I was writing to keep the ministry growing and strong. I am grateful to you all: Nancy Steele, Steve Lyon, Amy Stuber, and Doug Childress. Thanks also to George Toles for his always encouraging comments and for sharing with me his favorite-jokes file.

Finally, I thank two men who first showed me the pictures of love in the Song of Songs, Jackie Deere and Craig Glickman. They also officiated at my wedding to Cindy almost twenty years ago. They convinced me of the need for a love for all seasons in my own marriage.

PART ONE

GETTING READY
FOR INTIMACY

CHAPTER 1

FINDING A LOVE
FOR ALL SEASONS

Bill had been married for more than half of his forty-three years. Reluctantly wearing his first pair of bifocals and more than a little overweight, he was struggling to keep up with a demanding job and never-ending yard work. Yet what ate at him even more than his subpar performance at work and around the house was how he was treating those who lived with him.

Bill knew he was sagging behind more each day in being the father and husband he knew he should be. His marriage with Susan had started off fine. But somewhere between three corporate moves and two children, they'd lost the flame. In fact, it was now painfully obvious to both of them that the love they had for each other was barely a spark.

There was little romance, and few positive words were spoken between them. On one hand, she was becoming an expert at explaining to the children why their father wasn't coming home before they went to bed—and why he had to leave for work before they got up. On the other, he was becoming world-class at dodging his wife's angry stares when they met in the hallway and hiding behind a wall of denial that things "really aren't that bad."

Many of the other men in his church had gone to a major men's conference and come back supercharged to have a better marriage. In a rare moment of emotional honesty, however, Bill found himself thinking after that same event, *If it weren't for the children and what people would say at the church . . .*

He shuddered to think that he could even dream of tossing in the towel and leaving his wife and children—but that's exactly what he'd been thinking.

What is real love? Bill asked himself. And at a different, deeper level, *Were we ever in love in the first place?*

What was it that he and Susan had walked away from, without even realizing they'd made a wrong turn? What could he do to pull his family together? To rekindle a flame that he knew God wanted for them? To build the kind of love that would have him and Susan standing together, hand in hand and heart to heart, at their fiftieth high school reunion?

Unlike Bill, Brenda was unmarried, though seriously interested in one man. Yet her questions were strangely the same, and she too was searching for intimacy, though her approach was different.

Everyone, even her father who had never *remotely* approved of anyone she had brought home, told her what a "catch" Jim was. Then why was she the only one having so much trouble feeling settled and secure inside? At age thirty-one, Brenda was intelligent, indispensable at work, actively involved at her church . . . and now engaged. After years of playing the dating game—and twice being the one who ended "serious" dating relationships—things with Jim had been different. She had accepted his ring, and her heart had soared inside when he proposed.

But that was two months ago. Now, with a wedding looming in the spring, those same, nagging doubts she'd had with past "beaus" came creeping back: *Is this really love?* She wondered if her love for Jim was just a feeling. *Without a doubt he's a godly, loving man, but how can I be certain that this is real love? Is it the genuine, biblical article?* Brenda was looking for some reliable standard, some objective way of looking at love. She wanted a template that could help her know if their relationship was based on passing attraction or the lasting commitment that had kept her parents loving each other through forty-plus years of marriage.

"Lord, can someone really know when she's in love? Can she know what real love looks like?" Brenda prayed this time and again. She longed for an answer that would free her to walk down that aisle more certain than ever that she was right at the center of God's will. But was there really an answer to be found?

The differences between Bill and Brenda were striking. One was male, the other female. One wondered if his marriage was over; the other looked with hope at a marriage yet to be. Yet both of them desired the same thing: *Each needed to understand in his or her own world what genuine love looked like.*

Bill and Brenda needed to see a picture of love, to put it through a prism and see its brilliant colors displayed. What's more, each of them needed to know that such a love wasn't just for Disney movies or the couple down the street. They needed to know that they could lay claim to such a wholesome, wholehearted attraction in their own lives. In short, they needed to know the same thing each one of us needs to know as well.

Whether you're married or single, you need to know how to find and hold onto a love that can last, a love for all seasons.

God Himself has given us a clear picture of what a godly courtship should look like.

You may be married, wanting to not just endure being married, but to experience the kind of closeness you know deep inside is possible. To look into your loved one's eyes and see them light up when you walk in the door. To have her respond to your touch without pulling away. To have him verbally appreciate your efforts at the job and/or around the house. Are there really guidelines to ignite or rekindle affection, commitment, and acts of everyday caring—even after ten years and two (or more) kids?

The answer is: They're right within your reach.

You may be single, looking for some kind of clarity about your dating relationships, and we want to build a foundation that is crisscrossed with reinforced concrete, not the sinking sand you see in so many friends' marriages. Is that really possible in today's throwaway society?

The answer is: "Yes, absolutely."

God Himself *has* given us a clear picture of what a godly courtship should look like. He has provided us with a biblical blueprint for understanding what genuine love is—and what fleeting attraction looks like as well. As a single person, seeking to make an incredibly important decision about a potential mate, there is a standard you can lay your relationship up against—a series of divinely laid-down hashmarks that can tell you clearly how your "love" measures up.

I realize that in the harsh world of "diversity training," divorce courts, restraining orders, and broken dreams, such clear thinking on genuine love can seem like fantasy or hyperbole. But the power-packed picture of love I'm speaking about comes from a place of seamless integrity, complete honesty, and unshakable authority—God's Word.

> *Tucked away in the Old Testament is a treasure trove of wise counsel on godly relationships for those who'll search.*

As we'll see, God's Word not only gives us the solution to forgiveness of sin and eternal life through His Son, Jesus, but also foundational principles on building a caring, lasting earthly love as well. In fact, in the canon of Scripture, one entire book in the Old Testament has been specifically set aside to give us a "picture" of the greatest human love story of all time.

"Old Testament? Maybe that's why I haven't heard of a book like that before. Which book is it?"

Tucked away in the Old Testament is a treasure trove of wise counsel on godly relationships for those who'll search. It was written by the wisest of earthly kings, and draws on additional wisdom from his best friend and bride. And yes, it does carry the designation as the greatest love story ever told.

It's a book with an unusual title, "The Song of Songs." The Song is part of what is called the Wisdom Literature of the Old Testament (which includes the Psalms and the Proverbs), and it unearths eight brilliant relational gems we can gather and put to use in our courtship or marriage. Those eight principles can provide a couple of any age with enough emotional, spiritual, and physical riches to make each new season of life as fresh and refreshing as spring. For example, in the pages that follow:

- *You'll learn the primary way to increase the passion level in your home.*
- *You'll discover a family leadership style that builds closeness and unity.*
- *You'll find a key to increasing (or reestablishing) security and trust in your spouse.*
- *You'll see how intimacy is inseparably linked to making an internal "address change."*
- *You'll be exposed to a primary tool for long-term relationship renewal.*
- *You'll be encouraged to grow closer spiritually than ever before.*

All that from a "song"?

With radio stations today playing music by such groups as Pearl Jam and 2 Live Crew, the thought of a "song" having life-changing significance may seem strange. But when you realize that this song was composed by a man God counted as the "wisest" who ever lived, you get the idea that what he has to share with us indeed belongs at the top of the charts.

Get ready to put on the headphones, push the play button, and listen to the "Song of Songs." It's a "song" about a love that can last for all seasons. And a song that asks of us something great.

CHAPTER 2

A PICTURE OF SOMETHING GREAT

What would you say is the greatest love story of all time? If you have read much popular literature, you'd have to consider such classic stories as *Romeo and Juliet, The Scarlet Pimpernel,* or *Les Miserables.* If you recall classic, true-life romances, you might nominate Grace Kelly marrying the Prince of Monaco or (until the curtain was pulled back on "Camelot") John and Jackie Kennedy. Others would hold out for current-day romance tales like *While You Were Sleeping* or *Clueless in Seattle.* (Whoops! Make that *Sleepless* in Seattle.)

While the world may argue over the list of nominees for the greatest love story, the award has actually already been handed out. In a quiet awards ceremony, long before there were any nosy press reporters or pampered Hollywood celebrities, the Creator of romance already declared a winner. It's an incredibly beautiful story of two people deeply in love called "The Song of Songs."

ROLL THE OPENING CREDITS

In chapter one, verse one, we read, "The Song of Songs." This was a song above all songs, inspired by God Himself, and written by "The King." Not the heavyset "King" who once lived in Graceland and allegedly has now been seen at local K-Marts, but King Solomon, the wisest man who ever lived.

How much better to get our advice on relationships from the author of love Himself …

Why is that such crucial information? Go to any bookstore today and look at the incredible amount of shelf space devoted to "self help" books. We live in a world that offers "wise counsel" on relationships in truckload quantities—and that's from a society that tells us God is dead and Elvis is alive!

How much better to get our advice on relationships from the author of love Himself, instead of Dear Abby or Dr. Ruth. And a quick overview of this life-changing "song" can show us why it's so special in God's eyes.

First, it's given *a song title like none other*. Second, it captures in "picture" form *eight ways we can learn about genuine love* and put them into practice. And third, it contains *an incredible challenge*.

AN UNEQUALED TITLE

When God calls this book "The Song of Songs," He isn't being redundant. Rather, He's being resplendent in His praise. For in Old Testament times, if you wanted to say something was tremendous, incredible, without equal or rival (or even "totally rad!" as my daughters have occasionally been known to say), you would double the attribute. For example, in the book of Isaiah, you see where this "doubling" effect pushes an attribute of deity to perfection. There almighty God is called the "King of Kings" and the "Lord of Lords." In other words, the prophet points out that our God is the King above all kings and the Lord above all lords.

Here, it's the "Song of Songs." In other words, the greatest love story of all time. And as the ultimate love story, or love song, it carries the full depth of God's Word. This is not the paper-thin counsel on love and marriage taught on afternoon talk shows but the prudent counsel of an altogether wise Creator.

And because it's a song based on absolute truth, it holds

the life-changing ability to slip beneath our skin and pene-trate all the way to our heart and soul. The Scripture puts it this way: "For the word of God is living and active and sharper than any two-edged sword, and piercing as far as the division of soul and spirit, of both joints and marrow, and able to judge the thoughts and intentions of the heart" (Hebrews 4:12).

What that means to each of us reading this song is that we'll soon find God's Word reading *us*—opening up the deepest, most secret parts of our thought life and private actions. In a sense, Solomon's Song is God opening our mail, exposing attitudes that we may write about and send to only our closest friends or family. God peels back the shiny veneer we present to others at church and shows us how our love really looks when placed against a biblical model.

Count on this biblical love story to challenge your attitudes and call you to a deeper level of commitment than ever before.

In short, count on this biblical love story to challenge your attitudes and call you to a deeper level of commitment than ever before. And it will do so by giving you eight clear reflections of what courtship and marital love should look like.

EIGHT PICTURES OF GENUINE INTIMACY

The eight reflections of genuine love could be called "pic-tures," because that's exactly what Solomon gives us through-out Song of Songs. From beginning to end, this wisest of all men compresses the concepts he wants to share into picture form. Not because we're too dense to pick up everyday lan-guage, but because he's wise enough to know that pictures communicate on a much deeper level. These pictures reflect key ways to nurture intimacy with the person we love.

Understanding Solomon and his bride's use of pictures is a key to understanding the powerful principles they convey.

We'll talk more about understanding "pictorial language" in the next chapter, but for now here's a brief overview of these eight "pictures" and how they give us a clear look at a God-honored courtship and marriage:

1. A *Picture of* Inner Attraction

It may surprise you, but the major element that elevates his bride's passion level is not Solomon's bank account, biceps, or power to get things done. Boiled down to basics, it's his inner character that attracts her. It's his "name," or reputation, poured through a filtering process, that excites and maintains her desire for him. In this chapter, we'll see how a life that honors God is the best way to promote marital passion. And we'll see several specifics on how becoming a person of high character can establish a passionate, romance-filled marriage. We call this *a purified character*.

2. A *Picture of* Practiced Praise

In the realities of a fallen world, many people enter into marriage with a deep sense of insecurity and a low sense of worth to God or others. That nagging sense of low worth can cause even Christians to "live up" to the low opinion of themselves—causing major relationship problems down the road. Is there a biblical way of addressing this problem?

Absolutely. In the next three pictures of love, Solomon and his bride illustrate three specific ways of moving someone we love from insecurity to ever deepening security, from feeling shaky about where they stand to having rock-solid certainty of their spouse's love and their own God-given worth. Here we'll discover a powerful communication tool, a *specific* way to help a loved one not only hear that he or she is loved, but begin to feel and believe it deep inside. We call this *practicing praise*.

3. A *Picture of* Walking Toward Closeness

Far too often, couples are blocked from ever gaining the intimate relationship they want. Why? Because they've missed a crucial first step toward closeness. Before a couple can truly move together, they must move *away* from their parents and past. Much more than just moving out, men and women of any age can carve out a biblical, honoring independence. We'll see how to "leave" even those hard-to-leave homes that can block our ability to "cleave" to our spouse (Genesis 2: 24). We call this *leaving home*.

4. A *Picture of* Facing *"Pint-Sized"* Predators

With a wisdom that matches her husband's, the bride in Song of Songs calls on him to use his "hunting" skills to track down small predators that could harm their relationship. From anger, to procrastination, to a lack of consistently taking in spiritual nourishment, small things in a relationship can later become huge problems. In this picture of love, we'll see a pattern for protecting our relationship by actively keeping minor issues from becoming major ones. We call this picture *chasing predators*.

5. A *Picture of* Sanctioned *Intimacy*

A key benefit of the marriage relationship is experiencing the physical privileges and passions of the marital union. Far from being silent on this issue, God gives us a beautiful picture of physical love through the eyes of Solomon and his bride. Not only will we "see" clearly how God views the sexual union, but we'll learn how this important aspect of affection and caring can become even more fulfilling and enjoyable in our marriage. We call this picture *enjoying physical intimacy*.

6. A *Picture of* Active *Involvement*

The sixth picture involves adopting a powerful model for leadership in the home. For Solomon and his bride-to-be, their relationship doesn't diminish either person's strengths, but actually draws them together. That relationship continues in their marriage. A look at this picture can show us what leadership in marriage should look like up close, how it can protect a couple from the "passive man/wild woman" syndrome, and what unmistakable benefits come when "two run together." We call this *leadership that draws two together*.

7. A *Picture of a Strong Building*

Solomon and his bride know something that today's pop psychology fails to recognize. Namely, you can master every in-vogue communication technique and follow every motivational speaker's advice for "supercharging" your relationship and still see it weaken and crack before your eyes. That's because cracks in the walls of a relationship signal a far deeper problem—a shifting foundation.

In this seventh look at biblical love, we'll see the only lasting, unshakable foundation for building a marriage that lasts for all seasons. Even more, we'll be challenged to look at what supports our relationship now, and what materials we can use to pass God's final building "code." We call this *building according to code*.

8. A *Picture of "Renewable" Love*

Our final look at this snapshot album of biblical love will show us an important way for maintaining the closeness we've worked so hard to nurture. It involves facing the reality that we all live in a world that will set our schedule for us if we don't set it ourselves. It also gives a clear picture of an important, yet seemingly paradoxical way to "spontaneously" rekindle love's flame: focusing on advanced planning. We call this picture *planned spontaneity*.

A CALL TO DO SOMETHING GREAT

Take a "song" with a title like none other, toss in eight much needed pictures of biblical love, mix them in with practical "how to's" and opportunities for couple and group discussion, and you have a recipe for what we'll discover in this book—a love for all seasons. As you take the time individually, as a couple, or as a small group to study these pictures of love, you'll certainly be setting the stage to enrich your own relationship. Yet you'll also be responding to an equally important call to greatness. Let me explain with a true story about America's sixteenth president.

During the Civil War, President Abraham Lincoln took to attending a midweek church service. During those terrible days of sacrifice and sorrow for both the North and South, this short time of praise, prayer, and teaching offered comfort and solace to Lincoln's soul. On those Wednesday nights, the president of the United States and an aide who accompanied him would quietly, unobtrusively slip through a side door of the New York Presbyterian Church. More often than not, other people in the congregation were not even aware of his presence.

One night, apparently deeply moved by the message and time of worship, Lincoln stayed seated until long after the rest of the parishioners had left. Finally, breaking the silence, the adjutant who had accompanied Lincoln leaned over and asked him, "Mr. President, what did you think of the sermon?"

After contemplating the question, Lincoln answered, "I thought it was well thought through, powerfully delivered, and very eloquent."

"Then you thought it was a *great* sermon," his companion replied.

"No," said Lincoln. "I thought it failed.

"It failed because the pastor did not ask of us something great."[1]

> *Each clear reflection of biblical love will challenge you to move toward a great marriage—not just a good one.*

Let me assure you that the message you're about to hear from this "song" and these eight "pictures" that follow won't fail because they don't ask of you something great. Each clear reflection of biblical love will challenge you to move toward a *great* marriage—not just a good one. Each look at biblical love will call for a greater degree of closeness and intimacy, so that we would not settle for marital mediocrity.

But you don't understand, Trent, you may be thinking. *My marriage is so bad, I'd settle for mediocre right now!*

If that's your situation, take heart. *Bad marriages* can *become good marriages, and good marriages can become even better.* In more than twenty years of counseling couples I've found that to be true over and over. Even if you believe your marriage is near "the point of no return" right now, *don't give up.* Time and again I've seen couples who had considered their situation hopeless find a "hopeful future" and a place of forgiveness and genuine love.

I remember one husband and wife who came to my office and began the session by literally *spitting* on each other. This couple reluctantly began to practice these eight principles and, to their amazement (and truthfully, mine as well), rekindled a deep, intimate love for each other. Today, after five years of living out these principles, they are closer to each other—and to God—than ever before.

I've also seen hundreds of couples who have good marriages make their relationships even better as they follow these eight steps. And in the premarital classes I've taught for almost two decades, I've watched engaged couples make major midcourse corrections that have salvaged their courtship and very likely kept their subsequent marriage out of the counselor's office.

GUIDELINES FOR LISTENING TO THE SONG OF SONGS

Whatever your situation, tuning in to the Song of Songs can help you discover more of God's best. But before you push the "play" button, let me make three strong suggestions.

First, if at all possible, make the reading of this book a "tag-team" affair with your spouse, fiancée, or the person you're dating. (Please pick only one of the above!) If your loved one won't sign on right now to read this book with you, then don't despair.

If anything, it makes it even more important for *you* to look at and begin to live out these eight lifestyle principles yourself. Instead of lamenting the fact that you're the only one paddling the canoe, realize that God has entrusted you with a significant opportunity. By applying these principles, you've got the paddle in your hands, and often you can begin steering your relationship toward beneficial, life-giving waters.[2]

Second, don't feel like you have to speed through all eight principles in record time. In a world bent on catching "hurry sickness," it would be far better to kick off your shoes, sit down with each principle, and slowly reflect on it. That's why we've included a helpful Intimacy Inventory in the final chapter and a study guide at the end of the book that can help you think through specific applications and insights for your relationship.

Finally, realize that you're about to discover more than just a few communication techniques or quick-fix methods for "tweaking" your marriage. As I mentioned earlier, the Song of Songs is a trumpet call to do something far greater. To *be* something much greater. It challenges each of us to be a more godly person and a more loving mate. To be a better example for our children, our siblings, and our in-laws as well. Even beyond that, perhaps the greatest benefit from applying these eight steps is that they can help each of us turn our homes into what noted professor Kenneth Gangel has called the greatest evangelistic tool the local church has today—"a distinctively loving Christian home." That can surely happen when you and your spouse are able to reflect these eight pictures of intimacy before your children, friends, and neighbors.

"Are you saying our relationship *can't* fail if we just read about these eight principles?" Absolutely not. None of us is immune from the effects of sin or poor choices if we start walking away from biblical principles. Even great saints in the Scriptures committed great sins. Yet I can say without hesitation that as I continue to work with individuals, couples, and families, I have yet to see a relationship fail where each partner is willing to consistently practice these eight steps to intimacy.

No matter where your relationship may be today, get ready to grab hold of some of God's most high-powered, transforming truths. The opportunity is yours as a couple to carve out a bright, shining love for all seasons.

Where does all this begin? We start by focusing on a woman's passionate request to be kissed—and the surprising reason behind it.

PART TWO
EIGHT WAYS TO NURTURE INTIMACY

CHAPTER 3

Principle #1
A PURIFIED CHARACTER

Remember the psychedelic 1960s and early 1970s? One friend of mine, who in his pre-Christian days walked on the wild side, likes to say, "If you can remember the 1960s—you weren't there!" But for most of us who do remember (even if it's just in picture albums of our parents), we may see strange fashions: browns and oranges and madras patterns, tie-dye shirts, and, if you stretch your memory, those extra-extra-wide bell-bottom pants.

During those turbulent days of free love in San Francisco and firefights in Vietnam, I went to college and can remember doing something that had my friends marveling. Somehow I managed to get a date with a young lady on campus who was in the unofficial Beauty Queen category. I'd like to say she accepted my invitation just to be around my captivating personality. However, my having inside connections to two tickets to a movie premiere just might have influenced her decision.

When the word got out, I think the entire wing of my dorm was as excited as I was for my big date. The day finally came, and I wanted everything to be perfect. I got up early and washed my truck, got a haircut, and then took my clothes to the local "washateria." Nearly two hours before I picked her up, I was decked out in my favorite brown shoes with the extra-thick heels, a cool madras shirt, and, of course, that new addition to my wardrobe: a pair of extra-extra-wide bell-bottoms.

To the envy of my friends and roommate, I left the dorm for my dream date, picked up the Beauty Queen, and we headed to the movie. The first thing to go wrong was that she insisted on calling me "Jim." Now, I like the name Jim, and it's close to John, so I decided not to embarrass her by telling her that she had my name wrong. Then, even though I had gotten tickets to the movie, I didn't realize that we would still have to stand in line. Make that the longest line I had ever seen in my life!

For at least an hour we stood in the line with everyone who already had their tickets. Finally, we began to slowly move forward. We'd walk two feet, then stand still. Walk a few more feet, then stand still . . . and that's when it happened!

As we neared the theater entrance, I felt something inside my pants brushing up against the inside of my leg. I quickly reached down to make sure it wasn't a giant insect that had crawled up under my bell-bottoms. Unfortunately, what I discovered was actually something worse, something *much* worse.

As I mentioned, late that afternoon I had washed these new pants at the laundromat. Like the typical college guy, I decided, "Why waste time separating the clothes?" So I threw everything I had into the same washing machine and then tossed them all in the dryer.

But something happened in the dryer that would leave me high and dry with my date. Two terrible words describe it: *static cling*. During the drying cycle somehow a pair of my underwear had found their way high inside the flared "bell" of my new bell-bottoms! (For months afterwards I can remember saying, "Lord, why couldn't it have been a pair of socks?") The extra-wide taper was so wide I hadn't noticed them lodging high in the "bell" as I put on my pants. But now, what I was feeling on my leg was the static cling beginning to loosen—and the underwear beginning to slide down my leg!

Finally the underpants completed their descent and rested on my left shoe. Imagine my horror! Here I was, walking into a theater with a beautiful girl, getting ready to watch an epic movie, and suddenly I had a pair of underwear on my left shoe. And she was standing on my left! As inconspicuously as I could, I tried to get her to shift sides so I could shake the underwear off my foot. But just when I got them off my shoe and pushed them to the side, the lady behind me utters a "Yuuukk!" really loud, and the guy with her says, "Hey, buddy, did you just lose your underwear?"

Needless to say, that was my one and only date with the Beauty Queen. The only positive thing about the evening was that at least she went back to her dorm and told all her friends about a dweeb named "Jim."

In a marriage or courtship, there are certain things we can do that are almost guaranteed to ignite a fire within a loved one. On the other hand, there are other things (like wearing underwear on your foot) that can guarantee exactly the opposite effect. As we look at the first principle of a lasting love, we learn how to add excitement to our spouse's response.

STRONG PHYSICAL DESIRE

Just listen to how excited Solomon's bride is at the very thought of her loved one: "May he kiss me with the kisses of his mouth!" (1:2).

These aren't the opening words of a Harlequin romance but the divinely inspired Word of God! In chapter 1 of this song for lovers, Solomon and his future bride are in the season of their courtship. And in an expression of unashamed passion, a "soon-to-be" bride asks her "almost" husband for not just one kiss, but many.

For almost any husband today, hearing his bride utter words like that would instantly invoke a "Yes, Lord, and may it be so!" Or, as an old country friend would say, "If talk like that won't light your fire, then the woods are wet!"

While we may blush at this strong expression of passion, God didn't hesitate to record it in this first picture of genuine love. Actually, it's a picture with a "double exposure." First, it clearly shows that *strong physical desire* is a natural part of a healthy courtship and marriage. And second, it shows us that *noble character* is an effective way of maintaining or even increasing that level of desire through each new season of life.

PERFECTLY PERMISSIBLE PASSION

Based on what we've seen already in Song of Songs (and we're only on the second verse!), let's set the record straight in our look at biblical love. There's absolutely nothing wrong with our heart beating faster and our eyes opening wide when we take our loved one's hand or hold him or her close. In fact, that electricity between a husband and wife wasn't invented by Hugh Hefner. It was created by our heavenly Father.

Several years ago, I watched Hefner, the kingpin of the *Playboy* empire, on a national talk show. As usual, he was making his well-practiced sales pitch against Christianity. He described a Puritan wife who was whipped in public because her husband caught her smiling during intercourse. With great authority, he extolled the "sexual freedom" that *Playboy* and other smut magazines had brought to our society. Then he insisted that this poor woman's plight was brought on by "the negative way Christians thought and taught about sex."

What a lie! If that were true, Solomon's future bride should have been horsewhipped! And if her unrepressed joy in desiring the kisses of her fiancé during their courtship would have gotten her in trouble as a Puritan, just wait until we look in on their wedding night (as described later in Song of Songs). In his rush to condemn Christianity, Hefner was looking at the misapplication of Scripture by one group of people, not the Scriptures themselves. Clearly, the Bible endorses the feelings of physical passion that find their ultimate fulfillment in marriage.

Am I saying there is no difference between the type of love that the world promotes and what's pictured here in the Song of Songs? Absolutely not. Before someone picks up stones and accuses me of saying the Bible promotes license, it's important to realize there is a great difference between

Hefner's incredibly costly "free love" and God-honored marital love. Namely, in this song for lovers, there is unquestionably strong physical desire, yet along with such desire came strong physical restraint.

While the desire to be kissed is present, it's not until their wedding night (recorded in Song 4) that they actually move beyond theory to the application of those desires. Sexual excitement was designed for the sanctity of marriage. Yet the message is clear. For engaged couples wondering if they're really in love (or married couples assessing the state of their love today), strong physical attraction is one aspect of genuine love. It's not the only picture we'll see. Nor is physical attraction anywhere near strong enough to *maintain* a love for all seasons. But the electricity between husband and wife is part of God's wise plan for marriage.

Clearly, sexual intimacy in marriage is meant for enjoyment. In Proverbs 5:19, we read that a wife's breasts should "satisfy [her husband] at all times." Here in Song of Solomon it's the *wife* who is expressing her physical excitement. Later in this book, at the end of a wedding night filled with intimacy, God Himself speaks up and says of their union, "Eat, friends; drink and imbibe deeply, O lovers" (5:1b).

> *The presence (or absence) of that God-given romantic spark is one way to assess the level of biblical love in your relationship.*

What's more, the Scriptures note that a husband and wife are not to deprive each other of intimacy except for an agreed-upon "season" (1 Corinthians 7:5). Why? Because regular sexual involvement by a husband and wife provides an important "protective" barrier against sexual temptation. Or as one good friend told his wife, "Why would I be tempted to go out and drive a Volkswagen when I've got a Cadillac at home!" [1]

Physical desire is not the most important aspect of a courtship or marriage. However, it's not to be downplayed either. The presence (or absence) of that God-given romantic spark is one way to assess the level of biblical love in your relationship.

But what if you're a married man reading this book and you've seen your wife's physical desires steadily *decrease*? Or what if you're a wife whose husband has begun to show little or no interest in intimacy?

PURIFIED CHARACTER AND PHYSICAL PASSION

In this same principle of love that begins the Song of Songs, we're given the primary reason behind this woman's strong physical desire. What's more, we discover how we can also maintain and even increase the passion level in our marriage.

Solomon's bride-to-be doesn't keep us guessing about where her romantic feelings come from:

"May he kiss me with the kisses of his mouth!
For your love is better than wine.
Your oils have a pleasing fragrance,
Your name is like purified oil." (1:2–3, italics mine)

Here is where Solomon's wife finds her passion—in the sterling reputation of her lover's name. In fact, this is the way to passion, for *a purified character promotes passion*.

Notice that a key word begins her explanation of what sparks her passion level; it's a small three-letter word that begins with the letter *F.* And it's something my friend and mentor, Dr. Howard Hendricks, always pounded into our heads at Dallas Seminary. "Men," he'd thunder in his trademark, gravelly voice, "when you see the word *for* or *therefore*, ask what it's there for!" Here, the word *for* is there to show how Solomon's bride clearly linked her passion level with her husband's inner character. She's responsive "for the reason" that his life is as sparkling as a celebration and as refreshing as a pleasing fragrance. (Obviously, he didn't wear musk!) But most of all, it was because there was something exceedingly special about his "name."

HOW TO PURIFY YOUR NAME

Her key statement is: "Your name is like purified oil." What does that mean? Some Bible commentators think Solomon's bride was responding to the *sound* of his name. In other words, hearing the word "Solomon" is like beautiful music in her ears. It's something so positive and "pure" that it brings a smile to her face and a sigh to her lips. And that's exactly what can happen to those in love—me included!

Years ago, when I was engaged to my wife, Cindy, I was living at my mother's house. It was the summer in between my master's and doctoral programs, and one afternoon I was outside making a minor repair to my mother's car. Working underneath a car for me is like entering hostile territory, because I'm a lousy mechanic who knows just enough to create danger. But I thought I could handle this assignment: straighten the plastic front-end guard that had been bent by a concrete block in a parking stall.

Twice in the first minute of my crawling under the car, however, the phone started ringing. Both times I crawled out from under the car, wiped off my hands, and took the receiver from my mom. I decided enough was enough, and said in no uncertain terms, "Mom, I don't care *who* is on the phone. I'm not taking a call from anybody, *and I mean anybody!*"

Convinced that I was now safely cocooned from any interruptions, I'd been back at work for all of five minutes when my mother came out . . . again.

"John . . . ," she said.

"What is it now?" I said, my voice full of righteous indignation (which, of course, 99 out of 100 impartial observers would have classified as selfish irritation).

"Oh, nothing," my mother said. "It's just that Cindy's on the phone. But, never mind. I'll tell her you're too busy to talk."

"Cindy?" I said, the tone of my voice turning from rock-hard ice to melted butter in a millisecond. "You mean . . . *Cindy?*"

Moments before, it had been an incredible inconvenience to crawl out from under the car to answer those other senseless "interruptions." But just the mere mention of my soon-to-be-wife's "name" and I couldn't wait to be interrupted! What a difference a "name" makes![2]

For Solomon's bride, I'm sure the very sound of her fiancé's name stirred her excitement. However, it's obvious from the text that it wasn't just the *sound* of his name that ignited her passion, but the *quality* of it. For her words, "Your name is like purified oil," illustrate two other things that would have instantly stood out to Jewish listeners.

A Name Represents the Whole Person

First, a name captures the essence of the person. In Solomon's time, a person's name stood for far more than it does in most cases today. While some parents still give great thought and significance to naming their children, others actually attach names like "Moon Unit Zappa" and "Ima" and "Ura Hogg" on their unsuspecting children.

> *Parents once understood that a person's name is a powerful way of capturing all a man stood for or all a woman could become.*

A name in the Old Testament wasn't given to honor a soap opera star or a heavy metal heartthrob, or to be a clever play on words. Parents once understood that a person's name is a powerful way of capturing all a man stood for or all a woman could become. That's why God would often change a person's name in the Scriptures so that it reflected more of who He saw that person becoming. (Thus Abram was renamed Abraham, Jacob became Israel, and later Simon became Peter and Saul was called Paul.) And here, his bride pictures Solomon's "name" as having been "purified."

"Purified Oil" Assumed a Purification Process

Why would she specifically liken his whole character to "purified oil"? She's referring to the purity of his life. In his everyday words and actions, he represented a "see through" character that didn't reveal major flaws and imperfections. In fact, that's the literal picture behind her words.

If you've ever traveled to the Holy Land, you've probably seen a demonstration of how they purified oil in Solomon's day. For those who haven't, let me illustrate one process that was commonly used.

A farmer and his family would take fresh-picked olives and mash them to remove as many pits, leaves, and sticks as possible. Then the farmer would pour the unrefined oil and pulp through a series of trays. These trays were stacked on top of each other, each tray filled with decreasing sized rocks. Thus, larger rocks would be in the top trays, then smaller and smaller rocks until the final tray held exceedingly fine sand. The top trays would take out the larger sediments, and then each successive tray would further "purify" the oil on its downward path. This filtering process worked so well that by the time the oil passed through each tray it would collect at the bottom in a cistern (a scooped-out hole in a rock). Presto! Pure, refined olive oil—ready for home or market.

Now let's apply that "picture" to her soon-to-be husband. As Solomon's bride views him, Solomon is someone of seamless integrity, and they are about to be linked together as husband and wife. Here is someone she can count on to keep his word and to walk worthily before his God. Someone whose language is crystal clear, not streaked with "blue." She knows she can trust him to do the right thing, even if she isn't standing next to him to make sure.

Like any clearly thinking woman, Solomon's bride wants a man who can give her a firm moral foundation to build a life and family on. And as any woman would tell her who has endured a husband who has proved himself untruthful or unfaithful, she'd be getting no bargain if she settled for less.

No wonder she's so excited about being with him in every way. He is giving her a fundamental building block for a great marriage and sexual union. She recognizes that Solomon offers her a life of security and inner strength that comes from a growing faith in God. That faith will be lived out in a life of character.

THE COST OF FLAWED CHARACTER

What a contrast to another man, named Don, who found himself in major trouble with his wife, Jill. Don knew that he and his wife had real problems. More accurately, he felt *she* had problems. That's because when it came to being intimate, the term "low sexual desire" was way too high to describe her level of interest. Certainly, there had been plenty of romantic fireworks during the first five years of their marriage. Yet now, as far as his wife was concerned, whenever Don wanted to be physically intimate, it was never the right moment . . . or month! And the reason, I later found out, was an issue of his character. His questionable conduct lowered her respect for him and that affected her physical desire for him.

After years of working for a local contractor, Don had finally begun a small service business of his own. The business was based out of their home, and while he was out making calls, Jill, like many supportive wives, would help out by answering the phone. With start-up costs high, and his client list too low, their cash flow quickly became a major problem. Soon, some of the least desirable conversations Jill was having were with unpaid suppliers demanding late payments.

Without question, making a business work is a tremendous challenge. There's nothing harder than trying to explain to someone why you can't pay their invoice that month. But instead of honorably and honestly facing his creditors, Don sought to cut corners until he could play catch-up with his bank account.

When suppliers called and Don would answer the phone, Jill began hearing him lie about a payment that he'd "already made." And not just the increasingly popular "It's in the mail, trust me" excuse, but exaggerated lies, like "I've got a Xerox of the check right here!" when she knew there was no reality to his words.

Next, she heard him bidding jobs at a reduced "cash"

price. Of course, there's nothing wrong with working for cash. But Don's offer to discount his services for cash payment wasn't made to save on credit or collection charges, but to cleverly avoid any record keeping that would require him to pay taxes. Before long, Don demanded that Jill herself lie for him, all in an effort to buy more time to work out his business finances. Eventually his buying time with creditors by lying and cheating would lead to unwanted problems in his marriage as well.

Although it may not score points in politics or professional boxing, *in a marriage character counts double.* As we've seen with Solomon's wife-to-be, it's a crucial way of sparking a lover's interest and increasing intimacy, whether we're contemplating marriage or completing our fiftieth year.

> *The average man has no idea how powerfully a woman's desire level is linked to his level of godly character.*

Don misunderstood all of that. He also misunderstood "relational bookkeeping." He thought the hours he spent working "for the family" would win his wife's appreciation. In spite of his lying and cutting corners, he was convinced he was making deposit after deposit into his wife's account, and each would yield her interest. Yet his lack of integrity was actually making massive withdrawals. No wonder he was getting an "account closed" notice every time he sought to make a loving withdrawal!

The average man has no idea how powerfully a woman's desire level is linked to *his* level of godly character. It's what the Bible calls a "good name." Boiled down to basics it means:

- *Cheat on your taxes . . . and watch her security level drop.*
- *Let off steam from work by screaming at the children . . . and see her desire for intimacy that night (and the next) take a plunge.*

- *Lie when you're out in public . . . and don't expect to get a warm, private response when you get home that evening.*

CHARACTER AFFECTS BOTH SPOUSES

And don't think that character only counts on the male side of the ledger! While we've talked at length about Solomon's character, we'll see later in this book that he was just as attracted to her inner qualities as well.

Make no mistake, a man's physical responsiveness to his wife may not be turned off as quickly by her lack of character. But soon it too will become deeply and negatively affected by a woman who isn't committed to integrity. Let's face it. Dishonesty as a political official may win an election, but it eventually will hurt a community. The same is true for a husband and wife who want a fulfilling marriage. Chronic failure in your moral character can short-circuit feelings of love by your spouse.

"But wait a minute, Trent. That sounds good, but isn't there more than one reason for 'low sexual desire' in a marriage?" Absolutely.[3] However, it's clear from God's Word and even current-day clinical studies that a key to *increasing* marital passion comes from a purified character.

The DSM4 (Diagnostic Statistical Manual: revised 4th edition) is the primary manual listing all the major "psychological" woes people experience. Over a hundred pages in this voluminous book are devoted to "sexual dysfunctions." And in those pages, the treatment plan that addresses nearly every intimacy ailment (with the exception of primary physical problems) involves doing two things. First, decreasing performance anxiety and, second, increasing trust in the relationship. How do you do that? Try integrity. It acts like weed killer on anxiety, and like Miracle-Gro on trust.

It takes a godly character to maintain marital passion. But before we move on, let's make double sure we know what a "purified character" looks like. And to do that, we'll enroll in a short course on character development right out of God's Word.[4] For a life of godly character is the perfect way to pump up and preserve marital passion.

CHAPTER 4

THE FOUNDATION OF YOUR CHARACTER

In our world of shifting standards and "I'm no role model!" role models, many people simply don't know what a "purified character" looks like anymore. This lack of values training causes breakdowns in all types of relationships, from marriage to the workplace. It's so widespread that my good friend Bill Nix has developed a major character development course at his company. As the chief financial officer (CFO) of a major corporation, Bill became extremely frustrated with the lack of basic values and virtues being displayed in the people he hired. So to combat the cultural confusion he saw coming in the recruiting door, he consulted the Scriptures. A dedicated Christian, as well as an outstanding businessman, he isolated ten specific traits that he wanted every employee to exhibit. His list included such traits as honesty, truthfulness, forgiveness, and accountability.

Then Bill took those basic concepts, relabeled some of them slightly to sound less religious so they would fit under the Equal Employment Commission regulations for the workplace, and designed an incredible "corporate values" course.

At Bill's company, every employee from senior executive to entry level keyboard operator goes through a biblically based program of character development. With the legal stipulations of not quoting Scripture, many people don't even know where the concepts come from! It's a program that sets forth a clear standard of behavior and has caused morale and productivity at the company to soar. Why? Because it allows people who work in close quarters eight hours a day, day after day, to agree on a set of core values. It's a wonderful way to put the "Golden Rule" back in the workplace.[1]

CHARACTER DEVELOPMENT FOR COUPLES

I can remember talking to Bill about his program and having the Lord suddenly tap me on the shoulder. "Wouldn't it be great if every premarital couple you worked with were on the 'same page' when it came to a core set of values? Wouldn't it make an incredible difference if those married couples who sat in your office for counseling committed themselves to a basic set of virtues that makes for a great relationship?"

The answer, of course, is "Absolutely!", for the starting point to a great relationship is a life of character. We've seen that in the way Solomon's bride looks at her husband. Her passion is increased because Solomon's life looks even better on the inside than it did on the outside.

A life of character is one of the best investments we can make. Here's why. In case you haven't noticed lately, our bodies are steadily obeying gravity and the second law of thermodynamics. (That's a fancy way of saying we're falling apart!) There's nothing we can do that will stop time's eventual toll. But what about an investment that is timeless, rustproof, and actually makes us look better and live longer too? Those are all benefits of a life of godly character!

When we focus on building up our character, we can actually look better to our loved one, even if our belt size goes up a notch or two over time. That's because growing older as a growing Christian results in the "inner man" being renewed "day by day" (2 Corinthians 4:16). We all want to look our best and be as trim and healthy as we can. Yet a lasting attractiveness—one that eludes each time-etched line, each extra pound, and every passing day—is based on character alone. It's tyranny, not "trendy," to *have* to look good in fashion clothing for our spouse to appreciate us.

The reason we're taking such a close look at character building in chapters 4 and 5 is because everything else rests on this foundation. Trying to follow the seven remaining ways of love without a godly character is doomed to failure.

The threat of failure in character building and the solution is illustrated well in a story told by my former Dallas Seminary classmate and friend Pastor Tony Evans.

WHERE THE CRACKS COME FROM

Several years ago, Tony and his wife decided to do more than just have the inside of their house painted. In several of the rooms there were long cracks in the walls that simply "had to go." They brought in a painter who bid the job, got the contract, and immediately went to work. He carefully patched every crack, then painted over them until the whole house looked like new. It stayed that way for a few months. Then the cracks came back.

Unable to find that same painter (I wonder why), they called in a second painter. After showing him the cracks in the wall, Tony asked him what it would cost to fix his "crack in the wall" problem.

"I can't give you a price," the painter said. When asked why, he said, "Because you don't have a 'crack in the wall' problem. *You have a foundation problem.*" The house's shifting foundation caused new cracks to appear after old ones were covered.

That's why character is so crucial. Trying to build a love for all seasons without a solid foundation is an invitation to see cracks show up; even the same old ones can reappear. The reason? Flawed character. So to do your best to make your relationship "crack-proof" (or to learn how you can make some important foundation repairs if they're already creeping up the walls), let's turn to the one place that can answer the question, "What does a godly character look like?" God's Word offers the basics in a few very understandable, very applicable steps.

GOD'S COURSE ON BASIC VALUES

Less than forty years ago, you could stand on almost any street corner and see in the everyday actions of people a pretty clear picture of a "purified" character. But ever since the 1960s, much of our culture has been lost in a purple haze. Today, if you want to be a person of character (and to teach those values to your children), don't count on seeing it consistently in our society. But you can always find out what it looks like by turning to the Scriptures.

Many places in God's Word teach about a life of integrity,[2] but one condensed and therefore very clear view is found in Psalm 24. Right after the famous Psalm 23 passage on the Good Shepherd comes step-by-step instructions on the type of "sheep" the Lord loves to shepherd. Here's what King David (a shepherd himself at one time) wrote in verses 3–5:

Who may ascend into the hill of the Lord?
And who may stand in His holy place?
He who has clean hands and a pure heart,
Who has not lifted up his soul to falsehood,
And has not sworn deceitfully.
He shall receive a blessing from the Lord,
And righteousness from the God of his salvation.

LESSON ONE IN CHARACTER BUILDING: LAY THE RIGHT FOUNDATION

In this short course on values training we will concentrate on five lifestyle traits. And the first key to building sound character is found in the two questions that King David asks (verse 3). Those questions are, "Who may ascend into the hill of the Lord? And who may stand in His holy place?", and the correct answer to both is found in a relationship with a single person. He's a man whose "name is above all names": Jesus Christ. The foundation for a life of godly character involves coming to Christ as our Savior (John 3:16). It involves seeing Him as the only source of forgiveness of sin (Romans 3:23) and as someone whose shed blood allows us to become a "new creature" in Christ (2 Corinthians 5:17). Those who know Him receive a new life with new capacities to love God and their spouse. And to complete the picture, a relationship with Christ also qualifies us to "ascend" and "stand in His presence" forever!

To go back to Tony Evans's illustration, Jesus Christ is Himself the answer to any foundation or "cracking" problems we have. He has become the "cornerstone" we can count on to build our lives—the only source of non-shifting sand this side of Heaven!

Don't skip past this first lesson in building godly character, particularly if you know you're in a relationship with someone who "may or may not" have accepted Jesus Christ as his or her Lord and Savior. If that describes your situation, don't skim over the next few pages. There's something you simply must face.

> *"Do both of you personally know and love Jesus Christ?" The answer to that question holds the key to both genuine intimacy and to eternity.*

No matter how nice or principled your "beloved unbeliever" may be, he or she doesn't have an unshakable foundation to settle back on. Neither does that person have the renewable power source of God's love to strengthen commitment or to stand the tests and trials of time. It's not that Christians can't fall into sin or walk away from commitments once they come to know Christ. But believers at least have a way of escape from that sin and the Holy Spirit prompting them to get back in step.

All of which brings me to a crucial question that needs to be asked if you are in the "contemplating marriage" category. "Do both of you personally know and love Jesus Christ?" The answer to that question holds the key to both genuine intimacy and to eternity.

"THIS RELIGION THING IS HER DEAL"

For those in the dating phase of life, there are no guarantees that an extra-close friendship with a non-believer won't lead to falling in love. I remember several years ago when I was an associate pastor, one young couple we'll call Steve and Amy scheduled an appointment to see me. Amy had attended our church fairly regularly and very much wanted the wedding service to be held there. So, as I do with every couple, I asked them the "K" question: "Do you *know* Jesus Christ?"

Amy went first and gave a crystal clear testimony of accepting Christ as a teenager and even of being in a sorority Bible study in college. Steve went second and scoffed at the very idea of a personal God.

"Let me lay something out for you," he told me in a voice laced with icy sarcasm and self-sufficient pride. "I don't mean this to be offensive, but this religion thing is *her* deal. Not mine. As far as I'm concerned, we could get married jumping out of a plane. A church wedding is something I know is important to her. If that's what she's into, that's fine. Many people have a *need* for religion," he said with barely concealed contempt. "But it's not for me. I'm just here to talk about the details of the wedding. I'm not looking for a sermon."

Usually I'm much more diplomatic in talking with couples. However, you could see he had come in with a prepared speech—one that staked out his position and defied any discussion. Now that he had laid out his purposeful lack of faith, he was ready to sit back and let his fiancée talk about candelabra, wedding cake, and special music numbers. He was willing to come to Christ's church to talk about a Saturday afternoon social—but discussions about his soul were off-limits. So, since he didn't leave any room for discussion, I responded with an equally direct answer.

"What you said doesn't offend me. I struggled myself for a long time before coming to Christ. I thank you for being honest in sharing with me where you're at," I told him. "You've been straight with me, so let me be straight with you.

With what you've just told me, I won't be able to do your wedding. In fact, I have to tell you that I really don't think you two should be getting married."

Without exaggeration, his jaw dropped open, and he sat forward in his chair.

"I'm sure you are both wonderful people," I continued. "But what you're contemplating isn't so wonderful. The Bible calls it being 'unequally yoked,' which is an old-fashioned way of saying that regardless of how much you love each other today, you'll always have deep-seated desires and goals that are like oil and water. Those differences won't grow less as time goes by and kids come along, but greater. I'm sorry, but I think you two need to put your wedding on hold until you're both on the same spiritual page."

You'd have thought I'd put a large tack under him. He came out of his chair in a burst of anger, yelling how unfair I was being. Then, just as quickly, seeing the shock in his fiancée's face at his rage, he modulated his voice and turned on the charm, proceeding to tell me, "Don't get me wrong. I'm not saying there *isn't* a God. In fact, I'm sure He's out there."

"You're right," I told him. "God is out there. What I'm saying is that He's not in *here*—in your heart. . . ."

There was a long pause as I let those words sink in. Then I said, "If you're interested *at all* in finding out more about the faith in Christ your fiancée has—which, by the way, is the most important thing you'll ever look into—then I'd love to talk to you. In fact, I'll talk to you anytime, day or night. You name the time and place. But if you're asking me to skip that part of God's Word that says I can't marry you two the way things stand today . . . I can't."

Not another word was spoken. Steve just glared at me, and Amy's eyes filled with tears. As I purposely remained silent, you could have cut the tension with a knife. I prayed the whole time that there'd be at least an opening of interest on his part to hear more and for us to meet again. Unfortunately, they looked at each other, he nodded his head at her, and they both got up and walked out of my office.

Believe me, there was no joy in Mudville for *either* team that day. That was one of the most difficult and unhappy confrontations I've ever had. Yet I couldn't compromise the clear Word of God. Steve's blatant antagonism for spiritual things and Amy's history of a genuine faith were another Exxon Valdez oil spill waiting to happen—and unfortunately it did.

When they left my office, instead of going out and talking about what I'd said, they went down the street to talk to someone at another church. The fact that they were married there in a few months made it obvious that their desire to carry on with their *wedding* far outweighed any consideration about looking closely at their *marriage*.

As you might imagine, I wasn't included on the invitation list. However, I didn't go unnoticed. I got a scathing letter from the bride's father chastising me for my "non-Christian" attitude and informing me that they were now "looking at other churches."

Less than a year passed before I received a second letter—this time from the bride's mother. It gave me no joy to read that her daughter had already filed for divorce. Apparently, there had been a series of major trials, ending with her catching her husband in adultery.

HEED GOD'S FOUNDATION FOR CHARACTER

Please understand me. I know many of you reading this book were not believers when you were first married, and now both of you know Christ. That's wonderful! The work God has done in bringing each of you to Himself is, I'm sure, nothing short of spectacular. Now you've got a secure spiritual superstructure on which to hang all seven pictures of love that will follow.

I'm also not calling on those who are now married to a non-believing spouse to leave him or her. My prayer for you is that you will see your beloved come to Christ, and soon! And if I can offer some encouragement, one of the best ways to draw him or her to the Savior is to reflect the type of love we'll see modeled here in the Song of Songs.

THE FOUNDATION OF YOUR CHARACTER

Yet character begins with the right foundation: a personal relationship with God through Jesus Christ. Therefore, *if you know two things*—(1) that Jesus Christ is your savior, and (2) that you're within a few months, weeks, or days of marrying somebody who doesn't know Jesus as savior—then you must know something else too. You're deliberately choosing to go against God's Word (2 Corinthians 6:14). And while it may seem like you're getting ready to build your dream house together, you'll be building it in a floodplain.

I've heard the argument made numerous times: "But that won't be true for us! Someday, some way, things will change for the best. After all, she is beginning to show some interest in spiritual things." (She sang some Christmas carols with me and my family over the holidays!) Or, "If I'm the one who bails out on him, then that's just one more 'uncaring Christian' who's disappointed him. I've got to uphold my witness!"

Don't buy into that! You're not the only person God can use to bring that person to Himself. Perhaps your withdrawing from him or her for a season will be the very thing that jars him or her into looking closely at Christ and making a genuine response to His love![3]

> *God lays down guidelines not because He doesn't are about us, but because He does.*

You may wonder, *But aren't there unbelieving spouses who dramatically change over time?* Absolutely. However, in twenty years of counseling, for every one person I've seen make major changes *after* the marriage, I've seen a dozen make no positive change at all. In fact, my experience has been just the opposite. What you commonly see after five years of marriage is a believing spouse who is spiritually and emotionally drained, looking in vain for godly character in his or her life partner and awash in more problems than he or she ever dreamed were possible.

I don't mean to sound harsh. But remember, the Lord Himself tells us, "Above all else, Guard your heart" (Proverbs

4:23, NIV). God lays down guidelines not because He *doesn't* care about us, but because He *does*. (If you doubt that, look up Matthew 7:9–11.)

This is the first lesson in character building: Have a firm foundation, established on the chief cornerstone, Jesus Christ (Ephesians 2:20, NIV). God's indwelling Holy Spirit can give you the strength and power to live a life as clean and clear as "purified oil." But first you must be able to say "Yes, Lord! I do know Your only Son, Jesus Christ, as my Lord and Savior!" At that point you are ready for lessons two through five—four life-changing steps found in the rest of Psalm 24. Interestingly, those lessons lead us two steps forward—and two steps back. They're part of our continuing class in Character Development 101.

CHAPTER 5

CHARACTER DEVELOPMENT: TWO STEPS FORWARD, TWO STEPS BACK

Once we've made sure our foundation is secure in Christ, then we're set to follow the four additional lifestyle lessons set forth in Psalm 24. They're all part of our basic course, Character Development 101. The next two lessons are actually two things we're to actively step out and do. The final two lessons contain two things we're to step *away* from.

If we choose to follow these four guidelines that are clearly in our best interest, then God even promises us a special gift of His acceptance—His "blessing"—today, and the assurance of His presence forever. Now that's a gift worth living for!

TWO STEPS FORWARD

After the foundational lesson of knowing and following God's Son, here are two more lessons from Psalm 24 that involve our actions and attitudes: what we say to others and what we may not say but are thinking. One lesson challenges who we are in public; the other what we think in private.

King David writes, "He who has clean hands and a pure heart" (Psalm 24:4a). By *clean hands*, he's referring to how we act when others are watching. With a *pure heart*, he goes

deeper to examine the seat of our thoughts, will, and voli-
tional choices. Each lesson represents a step toward godly
character, so let's look at each one more closely, beginning
with the importance of having "clean hands" in our dealings
with others.

Lesson 2: Step Toward Consistent, Right Actions

Several years ago, I remember listening to evangelist Billy
Graham during a televised crusade. In illustrating a point,
this great man of God shared an example that shows the
importance of having "clean hands."

Graham recalled being on a cross-country flight, when a
man in the seat ahead of him began to create a disturbance.
This particular individual had been drinking heavily before
he got on the plane and continued to drink as much as they
would serve him on the flight. Not only was he getting more
drunk, but he was becoming louder and more abusive to the
flight attendants. When they finally refused to serve him any
more alcohol, his anger climaxed in a torrent of foul language.

In total frustration, one of the flight attendants told him,
"Sir, do you know that Billy Graham is sitting right behind
you?"

The man whirled around and said, "Oh, Mr. Graham! I'm
so glad to meet you. I went to one of your crusades, and it
changed my life!"

> *Something to keep front and center [when]*
> *living a life of character is: People are watching.*

It doesn't take a telephoto lens to zoom in on that man's
problem. Any inner "cleansing" that might have taken place
at a crusade had been totally covered up by the mud and
dirt of shameful actions.

That's something we need to keep front and center if
we're serious about living a life of character: *People are*
watching.

Every day and in every situation, people are watching. That's a thought that shouldn't make us paranoid, but more principled. Because if we lay claim to the name "Christian," our life before the world automatically goes on display. It's there for our spouse (and children) to see on a daily basis. It's a reality when we show up at work, and even with those who get behind us in line at the supermarket.

The thing about "clean hands" is that they're right out there for people to see. We may try and hide them behind our back, but it doesn't work. In the everyday give-and-take of life, we have to use our hands. And it's in our everyday actions that we make our godly character (or lack of it) clearly visible to others. Again, that isn't all bad. Knowing that people evaluate how "clean our hands are" in business dealings, our choice of language, and even whether we give back that extra change to the fast-food cashier is a very positive accountability tool.

A good way to personally assess how clean your hands are is to ask yourself a question: "If a *60 Minutes* camera crew suddenly showed up on my doorstep and began filming my life from the moment I woke up until the moment I hit the sack, would I be ashamed to have them broadcast nationally what they'd captured?"

Of course, none of us is perfect; we all get our hands dirty at times. Even the apostle Paul was someone who, by his own admission, had "dirty hands" before he came to Christ. He personally participated in beating and imprisoning believers, and he even held the cloaks and applauded as an angry mob stoned Stephen to death.

Yet what did the Lord say to him? "Paul, I know your filthy past. But get up, clean your hands and start living for Me!" (Paraphrased; literally, "And now why do you delay? Get up, and be baptized, and wash away your sins" [Acts 22: 16]).

What's the best way to keep our hands clean? By using the divinely provided water of God's Word that Paul pictures in Ephesians 5:25–26: "Christ also loved the church and gave Himself up for her, so that He might sanctify her, having cleansed her by the washing of water with the word."

Take God's Word, and then toss in the additional scrubbing action of loving accountability (something we'll talk about at length in a later chapter) and watch the spots come out of your character.

The more we read, memorize, and study God's Word and then allow others to lovingly hold us accountable to living it out, the cleaner our hands will be. But taking the first step to keep the outside of the cup clean is just the beginning. "Clean hands" are a reflection of the second character trait in this passage.

Lesson 3: Step Toward Wholesome Thoughts

When the psalmist David links clean hands with a pure heart, he's going right to the source of our actions, attitudes, and thoughts. From the deepest part of who we are, our "heart" needs to be pure. For most of us, that's a pointed challenge to closely monitor what passes through our eyes and on to the depths of our heart. Only God knows our hearts, but eventually the inner character of our hearts will reveal itself in our words and actions to our spouse (Matthew 12:34; Mark 7:21).

Take Elliot, for example. He was a Christian with a lovely wife and family, a nice home, and an ugly habit. The bad habit began when he was assigned a beautiful female co-worker who flaunted her sensuality. Jane did nothing physically to spur on his desires, but the way she dressed and spoke to Elliot made him feel as though he were spending eight hours a day with a centerfold model. Unfortunately, his internal resistance to temptation began to crumble.

Elliot never actually touched or even talked at length with Jane. He knew the dangers of a workplace relationship, and he truly didn't want to hurt his wife and his reputation. Instead, he turned to something he thought would be a "safer" sin.

To let off the sexual steam he was feeling, instead of talking to his boss, a close friend, or even his spouse, and instead of praying for help, he started dipping into his home computer, locating dozens of photos of naked women on the unpatrolled Internet. Instead of trying to purify his thoughts and his life, he turned to "private fantasies," which soon turned into an addiction to pornography. What brought him into the counseling office wasn't a desire for repentance, but his wife's accidental discovery of over one hundred X-rated pictures he had downloaded onto their home computer.

We need to have an inner self and an outer self that ring true.

The Hebrew word that is translated *pure* in the original language of the Old Testament means something that is "genuine, authentic." It's the real thing, the genuine article. Whether it's with our "hands" or our "heart"—in public or in private—we need to be one person, not two. We need to have an inner self and an outer self that ring true.[1] That kind of life draws others, and particularly our spouse, to us in a positive way.

David pictured two steps that can take us toward a "purified" life. Now he shares two things we're to walk away from.

TWO STEPS BACK

"Who has not lifted up his soul to falsehood and has not sworn deceitfully" (Psalm 24:4b).

Lesson 4: Step Back from Falsehood

The first thing we're to step away from is *lifting up our soul to falsehood.* If the phrase seems a little veiled to you, let me describe its origin. At the birth of a child in Old Testament times, it was common practice to "lift up" the little boy or girl before the Lord. It was a symbolic picture of wholehearted commitment of the parents to "offer" that child up to the Lord in thanks and gratitude.

When we "lift up our soul to falsehood," it's like lifting ourselves up to a lie. In today's vernacular, it's "swallowing something hook, line, and sinker." It's to "totally buy into a lie."

Margaret was someone who chose not to walk away from a lie—to buy into it instead—and she paid a high price. Margaret picked up the phone one day and heard an offer from a stranger (who assured her he wasn't a salesman) that sounded too good to be true. If she could answer a series of questions, her name would go into a drawing for a major cash prize. Amazingly, she got the answers all right! She was told her name would be added to many others, and then a few days later, she got a call back saying she was a finalist! All she had to do to secure her spot in the final cash drawing was provide a "totally refundable" good-faith deposit that would be more than made up when she won a major prize.

In retrospect, Margaret should have listened to the nagging doubts she had a dozen times along the way. It sounded so good. It seemed so easy. And after all, they said her money was refundable. (*Right!*) Perhaps because she was trying so hard to convince herself it was true, at the prompting of her "friend" on the phone, Margaret even recruited two close friends to enter the "drawing."

Many people "sell out" to lies in their everyday life.

You can imagine the outcome. The money was sent to a nonexistent company whose address mysteriously changed in a few weeks. Margaret was out more than one hundred dollars and had severely strained two close friendships as well. Margaret sold herself—lock, stock, and barrel—to a lie, and it cost her dearly. She is not alone.

Many people "sell out" to lies in their everyday life, lies that rip at our integrity. *They won't know it's missing*, we tell ourselves. *I don't have to report this, the government already takes too much from my income.* Or we involve others directly in our lies. "My roommate's gone and we really shouldn't be here . . . but I guess you can come in and we'll just sit and talk." Or, "It's better not to tell them. It would only make things worse."

More than ever, we need people clear-headed enough to

recognize and reject the lies. We also need men and women courageous enough to embrace wholeheartedly God's truth. Make no mistake, you can't embrace God's truth unless you are willing to reject the lies. Once we've made the commitment to live according to the truth, then we're told to avoid something that also goes hand in hand with lying—we're not to "swear deceitfully."

Lesson 5: Step Back from False Promises

The word meaning "to swear" in Scripture has an interesting word picture behind it. It literally means to "seven" ourselves. What does that mean? Like a heavy-duty cord that is "seven strands strong," it means we're to make commitments strong enough to bear the weight of time and other people's trust. We are to step away from false promises and step toward a firm commitment our spouse can depend on.

All of us have seen pictures of mountain climbers who have tied themselves together. Some may think that's to keep the scared ones from running away! But really they are trusting each other with their very lives. If one climber falls, he can count on the others to stop his fall—because there's a high-caliber bond between them. No one wants the other to fail, so all are tied together, committed with their very lives.

In a similar way, we're to make the kind of commitments that can be counted on. When we tell our spouse, "Honey, trust me, I'll get around to fixing that side door this weekend," it should happen. When we promise our child we'll take him to the movies, we shouldn't put it off so long we use the lame excuse, "Oh, sweetheart, Mommy got busy. But don't worry, it'll be out on video soon." We need to be men and women of our word. We need to take promises and commitments seriously so that our loved ones learn they can count on us.

What have we seen so far in our Character Development 101 course? We're to keep our hands clean in our daily walk. We should work hard to protect our thought life in private. We should sell out to the truth and not give in to deception and falsehood. Finally, we should keep our promises.

THE BONUS OF A BLESSING

This short course in character development, linked with the foundation of a life in Christ, comes with a wonderful promise.

What happens when our lives become characterized by these four wise guidelines? Our name becomes like purified oil. And as David tells us, "He shall receive a blessing from the Lord and righteousness from the God of his salvation" (Psalm 24:5).

What a deal! We choose to do the very things we should do—from having a relationship with God through His Son to keeping our promises—and then we receive God's personal assurance that He will bless us as a bonus! Now that's grace and love! Of course, it's also the best way to live out that purified character that will draw rave reviews from your spouse—just as it did with Solomon's.

ANSWERING A FINAL OBJECTION

Before we move on to the second of our eight ways to a lasting love, let's deal with one concern you may have. For three chapters, we've been describing integrity and righteous living. We've pictured Solomon as someone who lived out a "purified" lifestyle that his bride so readily responded to.

But if Solomon was so "pure" in character, you may wonder, *why did he have so many wives and concubines?* Maybe (as someone has inaccurately suggested) he was so good at *this* marriage relationship because he'd made every mistake in the others! In other words, after a hundred weddings he finally got this one right.

While it's right to ask why Solomon had so many wives and concubines, it's wrong to think we can't trust his counsel. For when we go to the Scriptures, we discover that in Solomon's youth, he sought just one thing from the Lord—wisdom. God granted him his prayer, and he became the wisest person who never walked on water.

*Anyone—even King Solomon—
can walk away from God's best.*

But though we may know *what to do*, that does not mean we'll automatically *do it*. In Solomon's early years, he sought to carefully and actively walk according to God's Word. It was during those early years that he met his bride, the "Shulammite woman" pictured here in the Song of Songs. It was later in his life—after being visited by the Queen of Sheba—that Solomon began taking foreign wives and concubines. This was sin, yet the wise king chose to do his own thing, and he acted unwisely regarding women and marriage.

That means anyone—even King Solomon—can walk away from God's best. As the book of Ecclesiastes tells us, Solomon in his later years sought vainly in all types of pleasure, riches, and knowledge to find "fulfillment," yet he never found it apart from going back to where he started—humbly following God.

As we explore the seven remaining pictures of genuine love, keep in mind that each one illustrates *a daily choice we have to make in our marriage;* that is, if we want to have a love for all seasons.

CHAPTER 6

Principle #2
PRACTICING PRAISE

One communication tool in relationships is so powerful that it can move right past a person's defenses and boost his sense of worth and value. The tool is so easy to use that it's already an everyday part of your conversations, yet so potentially life-changing that the greatest communicators of all time have used it to rally masses and direct entire movements.

The tool is the practice of praise, and this time-tested and God-honored way of talking has a marvelous effect on those who are insecure. In Song of Songs, this communication tool lifts the spirits of an insecure bride. By practicing praise, Solomon fills his new bride's heart with much needed confidence and self-assurance. Practicing praise can enrich your marriage or courtship as well!

FROM INSECURITY . . .

In the real world of relational bumps and bruises, many people enter marriage with a less than ideal picture of who they are and all they can become. That's not a modern-day phenomenon. Listen to the words of Solomon's bride as she shares a high level of insecurity at the start of their relationship.

"I am black but lovely, O daughters of Jerusalem,
Like the tents of Kedar, like the curtains of Solomon.
Do not stare at me because I am swarthy,
For the sun has burned me.
My mother's sons were angry with me;
They made me caretaker of the vineyards." (1:5–6)

In these early words of Solomon's future bride, she sees the potential in herself in spite of her problems. "I am black *but* lovely . . ." There's potential there, yet she admits that it comes with the high price tag of a less than ideal past.

For example, she's sporting a dark brown tan that didn't come from "Sinai Sam's" tanning salon. It came from the working world, where she was forced to tend vineyards day after day, through the scorching summer sun and windswept winters. Though being bronzed and beautiful may win points today, in Old Testament culture her dark skin would set her apart from the cultured "ladies of the court." They hid from the sun.

Besides being a working-class woman in competition with the privileged class, she was hampered by a home life that sounded far less than perfect. "My mother's sons were angry with me; they made me caretaker of the vineyard." She wasn't just working to help her family make ends meet, but was being *made* to work by her angry brothers! And with the unusual designation "mother's sons," you can make a strong case that her father was either absent or more likely dead. (Significantly, the Scriptures in almost every case trace the genealogies through the father, not the mother.) These brothers could well have been wrathful stepbrothers or half brothers ordering her around. Sounds a lot like a version of Cinderella or the average 1990s home, doesn't it!

. . . TO SECURITY THROUGH PRAISE

What makes this story so compelling, however, is what happens next. Just listen to two statements she makes about herself, and then watch a startling transformation take place.

"Do not stare at me!" (1:6) his bride-to-be cried, knowing

that the baggage she carried into her courtship stretched from her sun-stained skin to a family life filled with squabbles. Yet in a relatively short time—listen to this amazing change: "I am the rose of Sharon, the lily of the valleys" (2:1)!

Now *that's* a difference in perspective! But why? What could turn a pretty, but insecure, servant girl with evil step-brothers into someone who felt like a beautiful rose, a lovely lily? It was a caring spouse who was wise enough to understand and use a way of talking that can bring spectacular results. Let's learn about this potential-filled way of talking right now.

This wise husband added sand and mortar to his bride's sagging self-confidence by giving her an unusual picture: "To me, my darling, you are like my mare among the chariots of Pharaoh" (1:9).

PICTURES OF PRAISE

You mean, that's it? All I have to do to see my loved one's inner stock rise is to compare her or him to a smelly animal? Well, probably not that *particular* picture (though in that culture it was actually a noble description, as we shall see). What I would commend is the *process* Solomon uses here and almost forty other times in this short, eight-chapter book. It's the same process that his bride will use *more than thirty times* to encourage and support him as well.

> *If you want to see the security level rise around your home, then consistently use a picture of praise . . .*

If you want to see the security level rise around your home, then consistently use a *picture of praise* to point out an appreciated character trait of your loved one. When you do, watch it push right past his or her defenses and into his or her heart.

In clinical studies, researchers found that using this "pictorial" form of communication sidesteps the natural protective barriers that insecurity automatically puts up.[1] We hear our spouses better, receiving more openly what they say.

In contrast, the more insecure we feel, the more we tend to put up inner walls to protect us from words that hurt. Unfortunately, those walls also make us more resistant to hearing and taking legitimate praise to heart. For example, try telling your struggling teenage child, "Sweetheart, I thought you did great at your tryout!" Then watch her come back with the ultimate disclaimer, "You've *got* to say that— you're my mother." Or praise an insecure spouse and watch a negative reaction, not the expected heartfelt appreciation. Like the man who told me he felt frozen inside after something his wife said to him. He had been to a marriage conference and became convicted by something the speaker had said. Trying to make things better, he decided to praise his wife in the car on the way home. Her response? "Don't you praise me. You're just saying that because the speaker told you to do it!" (The answer to this man's dilemma is found in chapter 13: "Building Your Life According to Code.")

Solomon might well have met the same resistance from his bride to taking his words of love to heart if he had relied on everyday words to carry his message, but he didn't. To give his bride a new look at herself, he chose picture after picture to illustrate his depth of caring. But not just any picture. Solomon would specifically employ mental snapshots that he knew were anchored in her memory bank. Things she'd be familiar with, like Pharaoh's mare.

"To me, my darling, you are like my mare among the chariots of Pharaoh." For his loved one, Solomon was adding depth, contrast, and color galore to his words of praise. That's because everyone in his day knew about Egypt's chariots. These horse-drawn chariots numbered in the thousands, and gave Israel's neighbor an incredible war machine. In many ways, they were the first "HumVees" or armored personnel carriers of their time. Yet in Old Testament times, every chariot was pulled by fighting stallions.

That is, every chariot except one. A pure white mare— chosen above all others—pulled Pharaoh's chariot. Can you see the picture behind the picture now?

Remember, Solomon's bride has revealed to him some of her deepest fears ("Do not look at me!"). She has fears about being too common, too everyday, too easily passed over to be picked by someone who could have picked anyone. What does he do in response to her worry? Does he say, "Oh, honey, *lighten up*. You look great tonight. Now let's get going or we'll be late for the party"?

No. Instead he takes the time to take her seriously. He addresses her concern with a "pedigreed" picture of a beautiful mare that says, "Just like that mare, you're chosen. You're unique and special to me. You're outstanding among ten thousand."

Real love takes the time to take the other person seriously.

Give your spouse or fiancé a consistent dose of legitimate praise—put in picture form—and watch it become a tremendous therapeutic tool.

Because this is a healthy relationship, Solomon's bride replies in like manner, with a "picture of praise" of her own:

"Like an apple tree among the trees of the forest,
So is my beloved among the young men." (2:3)

Just as skillfully, she gives Solomon a compliment that will quickly call up a mental snapshot for him as well. It's a picture that would tug at his memory of the many times he had walked in the countryside. But why an apple tree in a forest?

In the midst of a forest, all cedar trees soon begin to look alike. (Take it from someone who's been lost in the woods *way* too often.) But how refreshing to walk into a clearing and suddenly see an exception: a tree that not only draws nutrients from the ground, but gives shade and nourishment back to those who sit under it. A *caregiver*—not just a taker.

An apple tree has become for Solomon's future bride a picture of his ability to care for her—and she tells him so.

Can't you begin to feel in the pictures they use with each other the tremendous connection between the two of them? Perhaps you're still not convinced that pictures of horses and apple trees can add stamina and strength to your relationship. If so, let me tell you the story of a clothespin at my home.

THE POWER OF A PICTURE

During the seventeen years that Cindy and I have been married, only once have I accepted an out-of-town speaking engagement on Valentine's Day. Knowing that February 14 is not the best day to put long distances between loved ones, I sought to head off any ill effects of having to be gone by doing several special things.

I gave Cindy a large bouquet of flowers before I left, a card for her to open on Valentine's Day, and even several love notes hidden around the house. On Valentine's Day I called her from out of town. Then in case my absence had still left her feeling down, I'd arranged to take her to a very nice dinner on the evening after I got back.

Of everything I did before and after Valentine's Day, guess what made the biggest impression on my wife? (Actually, it drew us closer together than if I'd never gone on the trip!) It wasn't the flowers or the card, the long-distance call or the costly dinner. It was something I had forgotten about until I got back, yet in Cindy's eyes it was the main thing that communicated most clearly that I loved her.

The day before I left, I was outside, playing with our oldest daughter, Kari. Quite accidentally, I happened to find an old clothespin lying in the yard. (It *had* to be old because we didn't have a clothesline!) Almost as an afterthought, I picked it up and put it in my pocket.

The next day when I was getting ready to leave, I gave Cindy a small envelope, telling her to open it on Valentine's Day. Along with a card inside was the clothespin with a note attached, "Honey, you do a great job of holding everything

70

together when I have to go out of town," the note read. "I love you very much, John."

When I got home from my trip, I saw something that startled me. That nondescript clothespin I'd given her now had a magnet glued to the back, a heart drawn on the front, and was mounted next to the other really important things on our refrigerator! (Have you noticed how things that are really important to people, like our kids' drawings and the missionaries we pray for, end up on the icebox?)

I did more to say "I love you" with a wooden clothespin than anything else. In fact, I could have skipped the flowers and dinner and just given her that. (Well, maybe that's stretching it a bit!) What communicated the most was a picture of praise. It gave Cindy a tangible look at a specific something I appreciated about her, and it went straight to her heart.

Wait a minute, Trent. That sounds so antiquated. In today's world, what about doing something more modern, like recording a personal message on the answering machine or sending your spouse an E-mail message on the home computer? Technology is great, of course, but you don't need some "high tech" means of communication before you begin to praise your spouse. Answering machines and computer E-mail can't substitute for face-to-face relationships. And in the real world of eye-to-eye interaction, there's nothing better than offering a picture of love for your spouse.

"All right," you might say. "I'll admit there might be something to this business of talking in pictures. But I still have a problem with it. It sounds a lot like poetry . . . and I was vice president of the 'I hate poetry' club in high school!"

I'll have to admit, you're right. The pictures Solomon and his bride shared between each other were originally poetry. But don't panic! You don't need any special ability at writing or reciting poetry to praise your spouse. In fact, just use pictures, without poetry, and you still win your wife's praise. As they say, "It's the thought that counts," and your pictures and words come from you. Your spouse will appreciate them.

Be encouraged that anyone can use pictures to communicate genuine love. These snapshots (like a mare, apple tree, or clothespin) can be serious medicine in helping a spouse heal and feel special. This, I feel, is one reason why the Lord gave us so many pictures of His love to chew on:

"The Lord is my shepherd, I shall not want."
"In my Father's house are many dwelling places."
"My yoke is easy, and my burden is light."
"You are my rock and my hiding place."

Please don't get me wrong. You won't always have a fitting picture to frame your praise of your spouse. And you don't have to. Sometimes simple compliments can do a great job of communicating our care, as we see an aspect of our mate's character we appreciate. But in a day when so many have feelings of insecurity, you're best armed to battle those feelings with this skill of using pictures. No language of praise equals the power of practicing praise through pictures. That's why in this chapter and the next, we are considering the practice of praise with pictures.

Ready for "praise lessons" given by a pro? Solomon is our tutor in chapter 7, as we learn how to praise those who matter most.

CHAPTER 7

PRAISE LESSONS FROM A PRO

We've seen that Solomon's bride traded in her insecurity for a healthy sense of her God-given worth. This was due in large part to her husband's well-chosen words. Yet, it would be unfair to assume that for someone with deep-seated problems, words of praise alone could heal every hurt. There are times when deep-seated problems need to be addressed professionally. One man told me during counseling, "When we first got married, I had so many problems, I could have done an entire week on *Geraldo* myself." Yet the best way I know (after reflecting a godly character) to keep from seeing a professional is to make effective use of these pictures of praise.

An everyday dose of praise can help your relationship in a hundred ways. It does so by adding strength to your commitment as you focus on the positive qualities in the other person. It also helps to build up relational reserves so that when you do have to point out a problem, your spouse doesn't react like you've just slapped him or her on a sensitive sunburn.

> *An everyday dose of praise can help your relationship in a hundred ways.*

In clinical studies, couples who make a habit of praising

each other also tend to keep a healthy focus on the future rather than getting bogged down in the past. They're more hopeful and more purposeful. So unless you're being blatantly dishonest when you praise your loved one, there is almost no downside risk in doing so.[1]

With so much to gain, don't fall into the performance trap. Some mates argue, "When my husband (or wife) makes it up to a '6' on a '1 to 10 scale,' then I'll start praising him (or her)." Instead, look for the good in your loved one *today*, capture it in a picture he can mentally see and understand, then watch him begin to live up to it. Thankfully, when it comes to learning how to effectively communicate this way, we've got an All-Pro example of someone who affirms his spouse—Solomon himself.

In Song of Songs he expresses his love in picture form almost forty times. Sometimes he reinforces her beauty to her; at other times he encourages her character and potential. Yet significantly, one time when he concentrates his praise is on their wedding night.

The wedding night is a time of great anticipation, but for many spouses, it's also a time of high anxiety. *What should I expect? What does he (she) expect of me? What will we say? How should I react?* Talk about potential insecurities!

But at least they have their privacy. Now imagine what it would be like if a transcript of that night's conversation was released to the press the next morning. That's exactly what God's Word gives us here in chapter 4. But it is not a bumbling, mistake-filled night. Instead, it's a glorious night filled with intimacy, praise, and passion—all with the endorsement of our Heavenly Father (5:1). Let's listen in now to the first thing that takes place when the author of intimacy pulls back the curtains.

SEVEN PRAISE PICTURES

It may surprise you to know that before this husband and wife lie down together, Solomon lays down a foundation of praise. At a time when almost any bride would feel insecure, he will affirm some aspect of her character or beauty seven times before he even touches her.

Seven times! Solomon praises his wife seven times before he touches her. Each instance of his praise offers us insight into drawing effective praise pictures. Let's now look at the seven, and we'll see a simple, three-step method for shining a spotlight on our loved one's strengths. With biblical permission, we now enter the bedroom of a king and queen and listen in on words of love expressed in pictures of praise.

Four Pictures from Nature . . .

On that rose and honey evening, the first attribute Solomon praises is his wife's eyes. He tells her:

> "How beautiful you are, my darling,
> How beautiful you are!
> Your eyes are like doves behind your veil." (4:1)

What is he saying with this picture? Obviously, she doesn't wear so much eye makeup that her eyelashes are like birds flapping their wings. Instead, as the best loved of all the many birds in the Middle East, the dove represented several things to his bride.[2] First, the dove's nonaggressive nature made it a symbol of peace. (It still is, as it adorns the helmets of the U.N. peacekeeping troops worldwide.) In fact, in releasing a dove after the catastrophic flood, Noah was seeking peace and a return to normalcy. Releasing a dove also was part of a peace offering to God.

As Solomon looks into his wife's eyes, he certainly sees a peaceful spirit, and he praises that. Yet a deeper look reveals even more. Namely, that her eyes are a window to her soul, and in her soul he sees something—actually Someone—reflected within: the Holy Spirit.

The clearest example of the dove representing God's Spirit is found in the New Testament at a dramatic scene in the Jordan River: the baptism of Jesus. This remarkable event carried much meaning. Though He was without sin, Christ humbled Himself, obeying God's command and allowing John the Baptist to lower Him under the waters and raise

Him up. Three years later Christ would be lowered into the grave, and then would rise in newness of life. The baptism also signaled that Christ had officially taken on the role of the Messiah—the Suffering Servant. At that very moment in time, the countdown to the Cross had begun.

With so much significance attached to a single event, it's no wonder that something supernatural happened to commemorate it:

> After being baptized, Jesus came up immediately from the water; and behold, the heavens were opened, and He saw the Spirit of God *descending as a dove*, and coming upon Him, and behold, a voice out of the heavens said, "This is My beloved Son, in whom I am well-pleased." (Matthew 3:16–17, italics added)

While the crowd may have been distracted by the authenticating voice of the Father that boomed out of heaven, significantly it is the Holy Spirit, here in the gentle form of a dove, who alights on God's Son. Also significantly, the first thing Solomon sees upon looking deep into his bride's eyes is a reflection of the dove, a reflection of that same Holy Spirit.

The first thing Solomon sees in his bride's eyes is . . . a reflection of the Holy Spirit.

His bride's eyes reflected God's love in a special way that night. And interestingly, in one of the few identical ways they praise each other, she will later praise him with nearly identical words, "His eyes are like doves" (5:12). They both saw life in the same way! Theirs was a shared, spiritual reflection, reflecting their common spiritual foundation that is crucial for building character (see chapter 4).

Before Solomon utters these words, he may have taken her hand as they sat close together that night. Now, before they embrace, he begins to share with her many attributes and character traits he loves about her. In doing so, he has begun by picking out something from nature—a dove—as a symbol of her gentle, peaceful, and spiritual character. Now he looks to her experiences in the rural culture of their day for other pictures of praise. Here's the second:

> "Your hair is like a flock of goats
> That have descended from Mount Gilead." (4:1)

Of course, before we draw a picture of praise, we should make sure it's something that our hearer can identify with and is *common* to his or her experience. Few of us have been to Mount Gilead, much less spent extended time around a flock of goats. But Solomon's bride—herself a shepherdess—would know just what he meant with this picture.

He's not telling her that her hair is coarse and matted or that when he runs his fingers through it, it raises up a cloud of dust. (At least that's what happens when you pet the dirty white goats I've seen here in Arizona who fight for existence in the desert!) Rather, he tells her that her hair reminds him of the black, long-haired goats that grace the green hill country of Lebanon. As the goats stroll across the beautiful hillside in the evening, so the black tresses of hair flow from her head.

A dove and a goat. The animals keep adding up as we look at the third picture of praise he employs:

> "Your teeth are like a flock of newly shorn ewes
> Which have come up from their washing,
> All of which bear twins,
> And not one among them has lost her young." (4:2)

What is *this* praise all about? As a farmer, Solomon's new bride would instantly recall the picture of the ewes after their shearing. Once their woolly coats were washed, the female sheep would come up sputtering and shaking to dry off, like overgrown puppies given a bath. Watching these freshly washed sheep, clean but shaking dry, the shepherdess's face brightens with a smile. That's when you see a person's teeth—in the midst of a smile.

Solomon is not merely praising her smile, though. He's excited about something else concerning her teeth. "All of them bear twins, and not one among them has lost her young!" To put it bluntly, "Thank the Lord she has all her teeth!"

If you're keeping track, he's praised her eyes, hair, and now her teeth, and each time he's drawn on the natural affinity she has to animals to make sure she "gets the picture." Skipping to verse 5 and the final attribute of his bride, Solomon again draws on animal imagery:

"Your two breasts are like two fawns, twins of a gazelle which feed among the lilies." (4:5)

Here is an unmistakable picture of intimacy, one in which he combines a picture of beauty and modesty. He delicately praises her breasts, and he notes how sensitive and selective she is in revealing them to none but him.

Consider the gazelle. You don't see its offspring in the midst of a field in the middle of the day. Baby gazelles appear in the quiet shadows of last light or the first rays of early morning. Nor do gazelles go "off their guard" even when they feed. In other words, Solomon is aware of the natural anxiety that comes with her revealing that intimate part of her body to him. And he is glad that in her modesty she has withheld from all men this part of her womanhood.

Before we draw conclusions about why he concentrated on these living object lessons, let's look briefly at the remaining three pictures given on their wedding night.

. . . Two Pictures of Everyday Objects

From cuddly or cute animals, Solomon turns to two pictures of everyday objects as he continues praising his bride. He says:

"Your lips are like a scarlet thread, and your mouth is lovely.

Your temples are like a slice of a pomegranate
behind your veil" (4:3)

The next time you get the opportunity to mend a garment
or simply cut off an errant "string" from a shirt or blouse,
purposely notice how delicate a single thread is. Here he pictures her lips as being traced by a thin, scarlet thread—not a
huge hemp rope! And, her temples are colored with the blush
of red that marks that unusual desert fruit, the pomegranate.
It's a delicate picture of the healthy, natural color to her
cheeks—something that brushed-on rouge just can't match.

. . . And a Final Picture of a Well-Known Symbol

Solomon has used "postcard" perfect animals and even a
delicate fruit to describe his bride so far, but with the next
picture, you'll think he must have made a mistake. Just as he
is ready to slip the glass slipper on her foot, he seems to
shatter the entire evening! Just listen to what he says:

"Your neck is like the tower of David,
Built with rows of stones,
On which are hung a thousand shields,
All the round shields of the mighty men." (4:4)

At first, this sounds like criticism. After saying something
nice about her eyes, hair, teeth, lips, cheeks, and breasts, he
seems to be staring at her unusually long, skinny neck all
covered with scales, cysts, and goiters! And after comparing
her to beautiful, lively animals, he now says she reminds him
of a building.

Far from criticizing her, Solomon is choosing a well-
known symbol, one his bride would instantly recognize. In
some ways, the "tower of David" in that day evoked emotions from people like the Statue of Liberty does in our own.
In our culture, the Statue of Liberty has stood for freedom
and hope for the downtrodden. Even with all the problems
we face as a nation, just ask any soldier, sailor, or Marine
who has served overseas his or her reaction at seeing that

statue as the ship steamed into New York Harbor and safely back home.

A well-meaning spouse might say to his loved one, "Sweetheart, you're a beacon of light to our family. In fact, you're a lot like the Statue of Liberty. You never cease holding up God's Word, shining forth His light to me and the kids, and it makes all of us feel loved and wanted around here." In a similar way, Solomon chooses a national symbol to picture a character trait of his bride. The citizens of Israel had an "early defense warning system" as effective as our modern electric warning lights and powerful loudspeakers: the tower that stood high above the Old City walls. Similarly, his bride's character was a pillar of strength to her husband.

The image of "the thousand shields" refers to David's "mighty men" of battle. They were the proud and efficient Army Rangers and Navy Seals of their day. During times of peace, they would polish their shields until they shone like mirrors. They would then hang them on the topmost part of the tower. From those lofty heights, these shields could then easily catch any sunlight and reflect it in every direction. Residents returning to the city wall and seeing the reflection knew the "mighty men" were not using their shields—the land was at peace. On the other hand, if one morning they noticed the shields being pulled down in a hurry, it was time to sprint back inside the city gates.

The symbolism behind this tower is why Solomon uses this seventh picture of praise. He likens her neck to David's tower, because his wife carries her neck with strength and security.

Have you ever seen someone who was deeply depressed? Almost without exception, a defining characteristic is that his neck is bowed, his head turned downward. It may not be a conscious action, but it graphically symbolizes the emotional weight he's carrying. Not so with Solomon's bride. Her neck, like the "tower of David," pictures confidence, optimism, and strong character. What an honoring picture, considering the heavy demands she had in working at the hands of her angry brothers!

Now that we've looked at these seven pictures of praise, let's draw some conclusions. In particular, let's see how the three types of pictures Solomon used give us a modern-day pattern for praising our spouse.

SOLOMON'S PATTERN OF PRAISE

Walk through the crowded gallery of pictures that make up the Song of Songs and you'll see something interesting. Namely, every one will fall within one of the three categories he used on their wedding night.

His references to animals draw forth an almost immediate, positive response. Then, there are those everyday items (like the clothespin I used with Cindy) endowed with special meaning. Finally, he draws upon a well-known "symbol" that would have added an instant positive picture in her day.

Those three categories open up hundreds of pictures we can draw from in praising our spouse. We can praise our mates by using everything from animals ("Diane, you're as playful as an otter. I really like that about you") to everyday objects ("James, I don't think you see it, but when you get up to teach our Sunday school class, it's like an orchestra conductor picking up his baton. People sit up and pay attention because they know you're conducting a great lesson").

We also can practice praise through referring to positive symbols. "Sherry, I can tell you're the Federal Express of your office," Brian told his wife one day. "What I mean by that is when your boss 'absolutely, positively, has to have something done the next day,' he calls on you. You're that valuable where you work."[3]

You may be thinking, "But I'm not creative enough to come up with a picture like that!" You don't have to graduate from "Disney University" to come up with creative pictures. In fact, whether you realize it or not, you already use pictures in your conversations every day!

You may be jealous of an older brother, convinced that your mother treats him as "the apple of her eye." Or you may admire a roofer, telling your neighbor, "He's strong as an ox, yet he treats his workers well."

All of us have said things like, "She's a blue-ribbon friend," "You're my Rock of Gibraltar," or "He's got an eagle eye." There's no lack of pictures we can use with a friend or our spouse. The issue becomes one of taking the time to say such word pictures.

Can you remember the last time you praised your spouse —and what for? If it's been a while, start by blowing the dust off your spouse's praise diary and filling it with positive pictures. To do that, I recommend you stop right now and move from the study of praise to its application. Complete the exercises for this chapter in the accompanying Study Guide. Above all, don't give up! If you keep it up, over time you will see the same thing Solomon did: a loved one who grew in her (or his) security.

Biblical love adds security to each season of life.

As we've seen, early in their relationship Solomon's bride went from feeling insecure to saying, "I am the rose of Sharon, the lily of the valleys" (2:1). Praise does that, chasing away many uncertainties as it increases security for your loved one. Genuine, biblical love adds security during each season of life. That's exactly what happens in the way his bride pictures her security in their relationship.

Early on she says, "My beloved is mine, and I am his" (2:16). Notice the possessiveness there. It's the attitude, "He's mine! This one's taken!" That was during their courtship. Yet as time goes by, she shifts her words, "I am my beloved's and my beloved is mine" (6:3). Though only a few words are rearranged, they reflect a deep internal change of attitude. Now it's not her hanging on to him. Rather, she's become so secure she can say with confidence, "I am my beloved's." She's learning to relax in his love after hearing it pictured so many times, in so many different ways. (And don't forget, he's also adding security by a "purified" character.)

MOVING TO A DEEPER LEVEL OF SECURITY

As more time passes in their relationship, she reaches an even deeper level of security. You can see that in her words, "I am my beloved's, and his desire is for me" (7:10). This third time, she not only expresses the confidence she has in his love, but she's confident that "his desire is for me" alone. Now that's security!

Let me ask you a personal question: Is the earlier bold statement, "Biblical love adds security to each season of life," true of your relationship? In your courtship or marriage, has the security level increased appreciably since the two of you have been together, or has it headed downward? Does your wife trust and respect you more than the day you were married? Is your husband more confident around you and others than he used to be? Is your loved one's sense of God-given worth higher today because he or she has consistently heard your words of praise?

Before you leave this chapter and our second picture of genuine love, make the commitment to increase the security level in your marriage. A good starting place is to be honest enough to ask your spouse, "On a 1 to 10 scale, how well am I doing at praising you and making you feel more secure?" Whatever the number is today isn't the crucial factor. Even if your spouse comes back with a "2," at least you've got a starting point or baseline to work from.

Armed with his or her honest evaluation, shoot for a goal of raising the security level just one point in the next six weeks. That's moving a "2" to a "3" in his estimation. Then after six weeks, set another goal of making your life partner feel more secure by moving that "3" to a "4." Then keep working at it until you're in the "7 to 10" range consistently— a place where you can be sure your partner is hearing your praise and reflecting it in a more centered and secure way.

This second mark of biblical love makes people feel more adequate, valuable, and unconditionally accepted. My prayer for you is that your home will be decorated with pictures of praise.

CHAPTER 8

Principle #3
LEAVING HOME

High school was over, and I'd been up almost all night, first saying good-bye to my few remaining high school friends and then packing for college myself. Now I sat at our old kitchen table with my mother, enjoying her famous pancakes one last time before climbing into my jam-packed car. As I sat at that table, a flood of emotions hit me.

My mother had purchased that table when I was five years old. It sat next to a large kitchen window, with a commanding view of the front yard. For more than a decade, it served as the unofficial meeting place of the Trent family. In grade school, I can remember sitting there at countless dinners. There would be us three boys laughing and chattering about our day, my mother and grandmother scurrying back and forth to keep bottomless plates filled, and my grandfather quietly presiding over the chaos.

In high school, that table became the place where I could sit with my mother, anytime, day or night. There she would patiently listen to whatever "crisis" or problem I was having in school or in dating. That old table proudly displayed birthday cards as we grew older and solemnly bore the flowers we brought home from the funeral home the day my grandfather was laid to rest.

Over the years, more chairs began to empty. My older brother, Joe, married and began a home of his own. My grandmother went to live with my aunt, and my twin brother, Jeff, left for a different college. Now it was down to just Mom and me, sitting at that table one last time.

I can remember how well I thought she was handling that morning. No tears. No dip in her always present smile. Just that nonstop encouragement that has calmed my fears since I was a child and always made me feel like I could accomplish anything I set my mind to. Things like driving a thousand miles by myself to a new college and making a new start without knowing a single person at an out-of-state school.

I finished breakfast, hugged the best mom in the world, and confidently strode to my '64 forest green Volkswagen. Every square inch was crammed with "important stuff" for college—everything from my legendary record collection to my new, seldom-used razor. I jumped inside the car, fired up the engine, and drove off with a wave and a smile. I was on my way! Nothing was going to stop me now! Nothing, that is, except driving into the rising sun that quickly made me realize I'd forgotten one thing—my sunglasses on the night stand.

I turned the car around, drove back into the driveway, and walked in to find my mother still sitting at the kitchen table, *crying*. All morning she had kept a stiff upper lip, managing to hold her emotions in check at seeing her last son leave home. But when I walked back in the door unexpectedly, all that changed. There was an awkward silence, and then we both lost it. We sat at that table, crowded with memories, hugged each other, and cried and cried.

I can't explain exactly what happened that sun-splashed morning in the kitchen, but our relationship changed. There was no less love, no less caring, but somehow we both knew that this would be the last time I would sit down at that old kitchen table as a child.

Things had changed. And so it is when a couple marries as well. Chairs need to be rearranged at the family table. Roles change; or at least they should.

Separating from [our parents and past] in a healthy way actually opens the doorway to intimacy.

At the wedding reception for Cindy and me, I became aware that the chairs had been rearranged once more. I hugged my mother; tears of happiness marked that parting as well. I remember Cindy and me ending our honeymoon by going to Pine, Arizona, to visit her parents. Her father is a rugged outdoorsman who (unlike Cindy's mother) never shed a tear at our wedding. But as we got ready to leave their house and drive to our new home in Texas, in a *very* unexpected display of emotion, *her father* was the one who broke down and cried!

No doubt about it, there is a unique sorrow that comes from separating from our parents. Yet as paradoxical as it seems, separating from them in a healthy way actually opens the door to intimacy. So for couples *of any age* who are serious about coming close, it begins with taking definite steps away from home. Leaving home means changing your roles and modifying relationships. Solomon understood the need of his wife to fully leave her parents' home, and we must understand that need too. It is one of the ways to a love for all seasons.

THE LONG JOURNEY AWAY FROM HOME

Just before Solomon and his bride enter into the act of marriage itself, he gently asks her to push away all thoughts of her past:

> "Come with me from Lebanon, my bride,
> May you come with me from Lebanon.
> Journey down from the summit of Amana,
> From the summit of Senir and Hermon,
> From the dens of lions,
> From the mountains of leopards . . ." (4:8)

His bride was sitting right *beside* him. Why does he ask her to leave home and come with him?

Solomon is picturing a journey she must make. He picks out three literal "high points" in the trek from Lebanon down to Jerusalem. Amana, Senir, and Hermon are three mountains she would pass on her way to her new home. And as he asks her to draw her thoughts away from home, he calls on her to dismiss any fearful or disquieting thoughts she carries from her past as well, the lions and leopards.[1]

Solomon felt it was important to increase her security level with praise. Now, he further insists that their lovemaking be as free as possible from prior attachments. He knew that the secret to their being totally present for each other came from distancing themselves from their parents and their past. What wise preparation for a time of passion! Here is an important lesson for *any* couple today who wants a higher degree of intimacy.

So is it just the *woman* who needs to face the difficult task of emotionally detaching herself from her parents and her past? Certainly not.

A JOURNEY BOTH PEOPLE MUST MAKE

It's true that in many areas of life, men and women approach tasks very differently. Yet in setting up a close-knit home, there is one area they *must* have in common. In Song of Songs, the woman is called to "come away" from home. But much earlier, in Genesis, the *man* is told: "For this cause a man shall leave his father and his mother, and shall cleave to his wife" (2:24).

Both the husband and wife need to walk together in leaving their first homes. Only then can they hope to defeat what happened to Janet.

Three weeks before her wedding to Mike, Janet nearly called the whole thing off. That's because her soon-to-be mother-in-law pulled her aside and "reluctantly" told her how she felt the two of them were "wrong" for each other. Mike's mother wasn't kind but cutting in what she said. She did not base her observations on fervent prayer or objective reality, but on sheer spite at losing her son.

Janet called Mike in tears, and together they stood at a

crossroads. Mike reassured her of his love, but how would he respond to his mother's words to his wife-to-be? He could stand next to his mother and downplay or dismiss the event. Or he could join Janet in walking away from home.

To his credit, Mike didn't hesitate. He called his mother and confronted her with what she had said. She admitted she didn't have any reason for saying such hurtful things so close to the wedding except for a strong "feeling" she'd had. So, in deference to her "feeling," he asked her whether she would rather *not* attend the wedding. That comment brought a clear conciliatory change in his mother's tone and marked the first step Mike and Janet *took together* toward a God-honored independence.

> *Every couple faces two formidable tasks. . . .*
> *First, they must separate from their parents, and*
> *second, reconnect . . . at a different emotional level.*

Like Mike and Janet, every couple faces two formidable tasks on their "journey" away from home. First, they must separate from their parents; then they must reconnect with them at a different emotional level. In this chapter and the next, we'll tackle both these tasks by looking at four specific ways of "leaving home" in a healthy way.

For some couples, the journey from "leaving" to "cleaving" is a relatively short one, helped along by two sets of wise parents who actively aid in the separation and reconnection process. Other adult children, however, come from "hard to leave" homes.

LEAVING A "HARD TO LEAVE" HOME

What is a "hard to leave" home? It is a home that specializes in making the journey to healthy independence steeper and more rocky. To move out emotionally from a "hard to leave" home takes extra effort and an extra reliance on God's strength and wisdom. That's especially true if you come from one (or more) of the three most common "hard to leave" homes I see in counseling:

Homes That Erase Our Identity

Anna grew up in a home where her parents couldn't see "eye to eye" on anything. Unfortunately, her mother compensated for an unfulfilling marriage by making Anna the focus of all her time, energy, and attention. All that attention may have been positive at first, but at some point it crossed the line into smothering. She was so involved, so possessive, that Anna soon found her identity only in her mother.

The mother-daughter bond became *too* strong, so that it caused a major problem during grade school. Anna was always one of the quieter students, but still she had several friends she played with. But all that changed. As time went on, she began to act afraid of her classmates, and would even run away when a friend came up to play with her.

An observant teacher noticed her behavior and recommended Anna see the school psychologist. Her mother reluctantly agreed, and during their first meeting, the psychologist gave Anna a simple assignment.

"Anna," he said. "Would you please draw a picture of everyone in your family."

Quickly, she drew a picture of herself standing next to her mother, with her father at a distance, surrounded by her two brothers.

"Now I'd like you to draw a picture of everyone in your home, except you." When Anna turned in the picture this time, there was her father and her two brothers on the page.

"I'm sorry," he commented. "Let me clarify what I wanted. I'd like you to draw a picture of everyone in your family, *except you.*"

A second time, the picture came back with her—and her mother—left out. Can you begin to see what was happening with this overly enmeshed young girl? Anna had become so emotionally bound to her mother that if she left herself out of the picture, it meant leaving her mother out as well.

She was so smothered by her mother that any healthy sense of an independent self had been snuffed out. Her possessive parent had become a part of Anna's identity, and the daughter was incomplete without the mother being with her. In fact, being away from her mother just long enough to go to school became a problem. Standing on her own, without her mother there beside her, she was fearful of meeting or even talking with others.

Anna's case is certainly an extreme. Yet many people come from homes where an unhealthy alliance exists between parent and child. These people become so bonded that they end up with no independent picture of themselves left to draw.

If you grew up in a home like this, expect letting go to be more difficult. The invisible lines of loyalty set up by controlling parents can make every step toward independence seem like you're "selling them out." Like the woman I spoke with who had been accepted at an outstanding, out-of-state college. She called her parents to share her excitement and was met with an icy reserve on the phone. Fifteen minutes after hanging up, they were standing at her doorstep. They laid every bit of guilt they could on her shoulders of not considering *their* needs or what such a decision might mean to *them*. Further, they demanded she go to that *perfectly good school* within easy driving distance of their home. She did, with great regrets then and now.

For Anna and for those like her, their connection with their mother or father becomes so strong, they struggle to escape his or her shadow. Their lives become total reflections of their parents, erasing any sense of their own unique, God-given strengths.

Homes That Shine an Unhealthy Spotlight

For Bill, his extreme attachment to the past didn't put him into the shadows—it placed him in an unhealthy spotlight. Bill grew up "special." He was the first child in his family. In fact, he was the first *grandchild* in the family for almost six years. That meant on every birthday, social event, or holiday, he stood alone in the spotlight. Many "only children" or "only children for several years" do perfectly well. But in Bill's home, the overboard affirmation (mixed with nonexistent discipline) proved poisonous. Bill became extremely self-centered, and as the years went by, began expecting and demanding attention from others.

Bill was athletic and attractive, and he regularly got the attention he was looking for. However, if one friend tired of doing everything his way, he was popular enough that he'd just switch friends! Like Narcissus of old, he had a tragic sense of self-absorption.

That's how Bill came into marriage, demanding a single spotlight, and it's the reason he and his wife wound up in counseling. He had dozens of specific expectations when they were married—all of them involving her cheerfully fulfilling *his* needs. And not just the domestic needs like cooking and cleaning; she was also expected to be excited about his every advancement at work, while he utterly ignored the successes she attained.

For example, when the opportunity came for him to enroll in a costly MBA program, he just assumed they would sacrifice the money they'd saved for furniture (and those other "nonessential" items like wallpaper) to pay the tuition fees. But let her bring up the idea of getting her master's degree, and he refused to even discuss it. It was obvious (to him) they didn't have the money.

Bill was so blinded by growing up in the spotlight of selfishness, he couldn't see his wife hurting, lonely, and wanting a mutually fulfilling relationship. Sadly, one day he came home to an empty house—his wife had left him—and he was finally forced to leave center stage and step out of the spotlight. Her leaving was the biggest wake-up call he'd ever received. With his charm and many abilities, he won everything he'd ever sought—including her. Now to have his marriage fall apart was a shocking, inescapable failure.

Fortunately, her leaving him also was a much needed blow to his pride that caught his attention. For the first time in his life, Bill was open to counsel. He took a hard look at who he really was—in and out of the spotlight. He started attending a men's Bible study and even joined a smaller accountability group. After a great deal of soul-searching, he began to put the Lord in the center of his life, and the needs of others in front of his own. Miraculously, after seeing the dramatic changes in his life, Bill's wife came back to him. His *actions,* not his words, had won her back as he moved from a life devoted to personal selfishness, to acting like a servant.

Bill successfully left this hard-to-leave home. He beat its relationship-killing power by putting aside the destructive selfishness he'd learned.

Homes That Violate Boundaries

Adults who were raised in abusive homes suffered either physical or sexual abuse (sometimes both). Abusive homes, instead of breaking the bonds of attachment, turn them into steel. For example, over 90 percent of sex offenders admitted they had been sexually molested themselves.[2]

One of the most challenging and chilling statements in the Scriptures is found in the midst of the Ten Commandments (Exodus 20:5–6): "I, the Lord your God, am a jealous God, visiting the iniquity of the fathers on the children, on the third and the fourth generations of those who hate Me, but showing lovingkindness to thousands, to those who love Me and keep My commandments."

There is great gain, for generations, for those who love and serve the Lord wholeheartedly. There is also great pain passed down . . . for those who do not.

That statement helps us understand why escaping from this "hard to leave" home is so difficult. Some sins are so powerful that they can penetrate the thinking of children, grandchildren, and great-grandchildren. They become part of an insidious pattern that is difficult to escape. There is great gain, *for generations,* for those who love and serve the Lord wholeheartedly. There is also great pain passed down through their bloodline for those who do not. That's not because God is a cruel or unjust God, but because of the binding nature of sin. From the very beginning, sin has sought to enslave and cripple like an out-of-control cancer. And it's only defeated by the One who defeated sin and death Himself, Jesus Christ.

Generation after generation, emotional pain can pile up when physical boundaries are violated. Hundreds of people can and do break free from these terrible chains, even when anger or abuse has been constant. Many of these people are "first-generation" Christians who, through the healing power of a personal relationship with Jesus Christ, have seen their marriage become the first generation of many to come who now pass down a blessing, instead of a curse.[3]

Following Solomon's pattern to "come away" with our beloved by leaving our first home may pose a greater challenge for those of us who lived in one or more of these "hard to leave" homes. But couples of any age can break past patterns. To do so, let's look at four steps we must take to fully leave our first homes and journey toward God-honoring, independent futures.

FIRST STEPS IN LEAVING HOME

At the end of each marriage preparation class I have taught at my local church, the couples (both engaged and those wanting to get off to a good start) complete an evaluation form. The teaching section that always receives the lowest marks is "family background issues."[4] But for those couples who have gone on to marry, somehow their perspective shifts. Along with other class leaders, I've hosted several formal and informal reunions of these couples, including those who have been married ten years or longer. At our "reunions," they rank "family background issues" *highest* on the list of topics they want to discuss.

What a shift in perspective! It's a shift that often starts when we find out we're not just battling present issues and problems, but inherited ones as well. No wonder it makes so much sense for Solomon to call his bride away from her parents and her past.

If you're an engaged or newly married couple, it may seem like the four steps in this chapter and the next will have the least "take away" value for you. But they will pay lasting dividends. If you're a married couple who has put a few miles behind you, here is helpful information on stepping past generational issues that may have tripped you up for years.

We begin our four "traveling tips" for those taking the long journey away from home with a trip to somewhere unexpected—a haunted house.

(1) Facing "Family Ghosts"

Mary had a family secret. It wasn't the kind that makes you happy, like the surprise party and weekend trip you're planning for your spouse's fortieth birthday. This was the kind of secret that makes you sad . . . like when someone has robbed you of your childhood.

Mary's grandfather was a pillar of a very prominent church. In his early seventies, he was serving his fourth term as the chairman of the elder board. In over five decades of ministry, he had served with many pastors and lay leaders who considered him their mentor and spiritual father. He devoted nearly full time to the church without pay. Yet on the side he was a child molester, and he had no remorse.

His crimes primarily took place against members of his own family, and Mary was one of the children who had suffered. At large gatherings, or if someone dropped off a youngster for "grandma and grandpa" to watch, he used his place as patriarch to take undue advantage. And while someone in Mary's family could and *should* have spoken up, no one did. The women and men in Mary's family kept a secret that became a family ghost.

A key principle to remember in leaving home is that many people have skeletons in the closet. The healthiest ones open the closet door, face them, and work hard to get rid of them. In Mary's family, no one was that healthy. The closet door stayed bolted shut until it was finally pulled off its hinges. That happened when her grandfather went outside his family one too many times and molested a child at their church. That family had no "ghost" scaring them away from confronting this man's sin. In fact, their lightning-quick response in calling the police and then challenging the church brought him instant disgrace and dismissal and when it was all over, a short stint of jail time.

> *Many people have skeletons in the closet.*
> *The healthiest ones open the closet door,*
> *face them, and work hard to get rid of them.*

Mary didn't speak up before this incident, but she did have the courage to be the first one in her family to tell the truth. She prayed about it and did testify at her grandfather's trial—for the prosecution, not the defense. By finally facing this family ghost, she headed down the road to freedom for the first time.

Are there any family ghosts you've been harboring in your past? A family ghost is something that's always there but never talked about. Scary things that are often hushed up by families include alcoholism, severe mental problems, abuse, unwanted pregnancies, and a host of other ills. They are part of our past. Though we can hide them, we cannot guarantee they won't materialize one day to terrorize us.

Family ghosts need to be prayed over, pushed away, and put behind us. In the Psalms, King David prays that God would reveal any "secret sins" in his life. Are there any past events or actions you were a part of that have stunted your spiritual growth and need to be acknowledged, confessed, and talked through?

If a couple is serious about "leaving" and "cleaving," it begins with a commitment to the truth. If you came from a wonderful home with beautiful memories, be open to talking about what your parents did right as a way of reinforcing those positives. If there were negatives, don't toss them aside until you've honestly looked at, prayed through, and talked through their potential impact on your life. Commit yourself to the truth—even if there are family ghosts to deal with.

Facing family ghosts and many of the other "traveling

tips" help us with the important process of *externalization*. Externalization takes place when we push into the open those issues and trials that may have marked or shaped us in a negative way. Once we get a negative experience in front of us, whether a painful childhood experience or family ghost, we can attack its power and influence over us.

Externalization helps us spot those elements of family background that we have forgotten, repressed, or down-played as unimportant, even though they continue to affect us—and often affect our marriage. An important truth to remember is this: You cannot dispose of something that you do not own. By externalizing an issue or past problem, we in some ways own it. And once we admit it's a part of our past (and that it's influencing our present), we become free to finally label it as something "apart from us." Now instead of merely "leasing" the problem and letting it remain nearby, we can dispose of it, working and praying to rid it from our lives.

It takes courage to admit and "own up" to a family ghost. But it's the first of several steps we can take toward an independent future and a walk toward closeness with our spouse.

CHAPTER 9

WALKING TOWARD CLOSENESS

Our younger daughter, Laura, has a favorite stuffed animal named "Special Teddy." (Named because it's special to her and it's a teddy bear—is she a creative kid or what!) Special Teddy sleeps right next to Laura every night, and primarily hangs out on Laura's bed during the day.

One Saturday when I brought something into Laura's room, I noticed that Special Teddy had fallen onto his side. I don't know exactly when or how I developed this problem, but I've always had the need to arrange stuffed animals in a way that they *look* like they're comfortable. (How can they *breathe* if they're piled on top of each other!) So, I set the bear upright and went about my business. Later that day, I walked by Laura's room and noticed Special Teddy was back on his side again. For the second time, I comfortably snuggled him back with his friends in an *upright* position—and within a short time I noticed he was lying flat again.

I knew Special Teddy wasn't lopsided. And while (like in *The Velveteen Rabbit*) Laura had loved off enough of his fur to make him "real," I knew he wasn't turning over on his side on his own. That meant that *someone* kept laying the bear on his side. As you might have guessed, that someone was Laura.

When I finally walked by her room and saw her doing it, I came in and we had a little chat. "Honey," I said, "is there some *reason* why you keep laying Special Teddy on his side? Wouldn't he be more comfortable if he was, say, sitting up?"

"Oh no, Daddy," she said, looking up at me with those beautiful, brown eyes. "He doesn't like to sit up. He's more comfortable on his side. He told me so himself. And he told me to tell you to quit standing him up!"

Never argue with a four year old who has gotten inside information directly from her teddy bear. And don't argue with the need to move your relationship with your parents from vertical to horizontal position if you're serious about intimacy.

MORE STEPS IN LEAVING HOME
(2) *Establishing a Horizontal Relationship with Parents*

Our second step in leaving home requires changing your relationship with your parents, moving to a more equal, horizontal plane. When it comes to teddy bears, you can lay them either vertically (the correct way) or horizontally (the way Special Teddy is most comfortable). Those two options are true in relationships as well.

The two primary types of relationships we have in life are vertical, known sometimes as "symmetrical," and horizontal, known as "complementary." Vertical relationships are fine in the right setting. For example, at work they reflect a top dog/underdog way of relating, like the clear chain of command in the armed forces. They exist in teacher/student relationships (at least before junior high school) and for mothers and fathers in their roles as appropriate authority figures with their children when they're young.

Horizontal, or *complementary*, relationships are reflected in the way best friends treat each other and in working partnerships. In these side-by-side relationships, there is more give and take, more eye-to-eye and shoulder-to-shoulder involvement.

Can you imagine what happens when—like what happened with Special Teddy—a "symmetrical" relationship gets turned on its side and becomes "complementary"? If you need some help envisioning this, imagine you have just received an unexpected promotion that instantly puts you on the same "level" as your current boss. Suddenly, the way you relate to the boss moves from reporting to him to relating to him eye to eye. Such a change can usher in some very interesting and challenging feelings and perceptions!

What can be challenging in the business world can be doubly true in the parent/child relationship. This change from vertical to horizontal relationships should take place throughout the parenting process. Your parents started by being much more directive and authoritative in your life. Ideally, as you grew older, they encouraged you to take on more responsibility, and they moved toward the roles of mentor, counselor, and friend.

It can be a challenge to relate to parents on a peer level.

With that in mind, you can see how a wedding can dramatically shift the way people relate. In a sense, as Special Teddy never (or rarely) has lain on its side, Mom, Dad, or you might get upset and demand that Teddy sit upright again! If you are not used to a friend-to-friend relationship with your parents, you (or they) may not want to leave the superior/subordinate relationship. Put in plain English, it can be a real challenge to relate to parents on a peer level.[1]

So great is this challenge of moving from vertical to horizontal relationships that the separation and grieving process has become symbolic in some cultures. For example, in traditional Jewish wedding ceremonies, the move away from home is scripted into the ceremony itself. The bride and groom stand under a "chupa," a canopy held up by four poles, each held by family members. Symbolically, the bride and groom are standing beneath their own roof for the first time. When the wedding ceremony is over, they walk out from under it to "leave behind the old" and begin to "build the walls" of their new life together.

In African culture, one Nigerian tribe reflects an even more graphic picture of separation and grieving. When a young man comes of age and is ready to receive a wife, there is a dramatic, nighttime ceremony. On an evening chosen by the elders of the village, every warrior stands in full battle dress, carrying a torch, and surrounding the hut of the young man who is "coming of age." They chant over and over, "Come out, son. . . . Come out, son. . . ." They're calling the "boy" within to come out and take his place with the men of the village. But *someone* blocks his coming out. It's his mother.

She stands at the doorway, trying her best to block his getting out, crying and weeping at the loss of her "child"! So serious is she about keeping him "at home," the young man must physically push his way past his mother before he can get outside! After a brief struggle, he breaks free and walks to where the men wait. Now, it's off to warrior training, and when he comes back to the village, he builds his own hut and takes a wife. (In the meantime, his mother is consoled by other mothers who have gone through similar experiences themselves.)[2]

What a graphic picture of separation! Everyone in the village knows that the relationship has forever changed from parent/child to parent/peer. How much healthier would marriages be in our culture if there was a specific marker event that said to a man (or woman), "You're grown up now," and to a mother (or father), "His childhood is over."

Changing the texture of the parent-and-child relationship isn't easy—but it's imperative. And one way to speed that process along is to make sure you learn to set clear relational *boundaries*—just like you would with a friend.

(3) *Setting Healthy Boundaries*

One important way to know if you've successfully moved from a "vertical" to a "horizontal" relationship with your parents is to ask yourself a question: "Can I set 'boundaries' in the relationship with my parents as I do with close friends?" Boundaries are limits to the relationship for the benefit of each person.[3]

Let's say you and your wife have a close friendship with

another couple. They're wonderful people, but they're *morning* people and you're night owls. Their idea is to get up at the crack of dawn—yours is to get up at the crack of noon! To top it off, they begin calling you every morning for weeks (*including* Saturday) at 6:45, just to start their day by saying "Hi" to their best friends. How long would your friendship last if you didn't set boundaries around their early morning intrusions? The correct answer is, "Not very long!"

> *Ask yourself the question, "Can I set 'boundaries' in the relationship with my parents, as I do with close friends?*

But, because they are close friends, in a healthy relationship you could calmly and lovingly tell them that their friendship means a great deal to you—but not at 6:45 A.M.! You could respectfully ask them to *end* their day by calling to express their undying friendship, not killing you by waking you up with those words. And, in a close friendship, both parties would come away from the conversation closer together, not farther apart.

What married children need to realize is that they must do that with their parents as well. A classic time to have boundaries is during the holidays, especially Thanksgiving and Christmas. For example, let's say your family has had a Christmas Eve dinner since you were knee-high to a grasshopper (as my grandfather used to say). You love going to your parents' home, yet now that you have children of your own, Christmas Eve is becoming a problem. It's great while you're there, but when you get home, you're up until three in the morning getting last-minute presents assembled and wrapped for your Christmas morning. Even worse, the youngsters get so keyed up and stay up so late Christmas Eve, they're major-league grumpy on Christmas Day! And finally, while your parents don't attend church, your church has that wonderful family-oriented service on Christmas Eve and you'd like to attend! What's a couple to do?

In a "complementary" (horizontal) relationship with their parents, they could muster their courage, sit down face-to-face and say, "Mom, Dad, we love being with you all during the holidays, and we appreciate all the hard work you go through preparing Christmas Eve dinner. But beginning this year, we need to switch our time we come over to your house. We'd love to come over on *Christmas Day,* bring the kids, open presents, and be with you all for *lunch.* But for a number of reasons, including our need to get the kids to bed earlier and because we want to go to church as a family, we need to celebrate Christmas *Day* with you, not Christmas *Eve.*"

Believe me, if you can say something similar to your parents, you're well on your way to setting healthy boundaries. And according to Song of Songs, you're also on your way to deepening the love of your spouse.

Boundary issues don't just focus on the holidays. They can surface in a hundred different ways. Like deciding how late (or early) a parent should call, or how often he or she can "unexpectedly" drop by without calling first. If your parents are not Christians, you may well have other boundary issues to confront, such as the use of profanity, drinking, or other practices you'd rather not see when they're under your roof.

Boundary issues not only are numerous, they surface at any time in a marriage. For example, Cindy and I had been married almost a decade when we had to deal with a new boundary issue ourselves. After years of living out-of-state, Cindy and I finally moved back to the Phoenix area where my mother lived. While we had never had a problem when we lived at a distance, now something happened that turned into a boundary issue. Whenever my mother would call with an invitation to get together, she would either call me at my *office* number or say a brief "Hello" to Cindy at home and then quickly ask to speak to me.

As insensitive as I can sometimes be, I didn't see this as a problem at first until it began to make Cindy feel uncomfortable. My mother and I were talking about our plans with little "front end" communication with Cindy, and she felt legitimately left out of the planning and discussion process. We had kids and I didn't know about all their activities; Cindy did and deserved to be an early part of those scheduling discussions. When she shared her concern with me one evening, I could clearly see the problem and took it to heart. Then I needed to take it to my mom.

The confrontation took place the same spring that I was writing my first book, coauthored with Gary Smalley, *The Blessing*. Using that writing project as a subtle way to approach the subject, I called my mother and told her a hypothetical story.

"Mom," I said. "I don't want you to be upset, but you know how I've been working day and night on that book with Gary? Well, after some discussion with the publishers, they've decided that since this is my first book, they're going to put Gary's name on the outside of the cover, but they're going to leave mine off. Now, I'll be noted in there somewhere—probably in the back somewhere—but I did want you to know that my name won't show up as the coauthor."

There was a long pause. She knew of my doctoral work on the subject. She'd also seen how I'd been working my heart out for months on the manuscript. In an explosion of angry words worthy of any protective, loving mother, she let her feelings be known about what she thought of that publisher's idea! I let her fume for a while, then, finally, I cut in and told her:

"Mom, calm down. I was just kidding. Of *course* my name will be on the cover." I continued, "But did you realize that you're doing something almost every week that is just like that to Cindy and me?"

She instantly wanted to know what she could possibly be doing that seemed in any way similar to my story.

"When you call me at work instead of calling at home, or schedule something through me without talking to Cindy too," I said, "it's like leaving her name off the cover of a book. Mom, Cindy and I are a team. It's like we're coauthors. So I'd like all of us to remember that, and to make sure Cindy's name gets included on the cover when you call."

There was a long pause, followed finally by an "Oh, OK. Thanks for sharing that. . . . Well, I've got to go." And she hung up the phone. That night, I was more than a little worried that she may not have "gotten the picture" or that she'd taken what I said wrong. But the next day, she called and spoke with Cindy. After they talked at length and laid to rest any misunderstandings, Mom got me on the phone and said, "John, I didn't mean to leave Cindy out, but I can see how it certainly looks that way. Don't worry. I'll make sure she stays on the cover of the book from now on."

That conversation took place more than ten years ago, and I've never had to remind my mother about that boundary issue again. That's because most loving parents, once they "get the picture" of changing boundaries, will often bend over backward to respect them.

For some of us, a stumbling block in our spiritual life can be a lack of forgiveness toward our parents.

It's important to define boundary issues with our parents and with our "extended" family as well. Along with each of the other steps we've seen in this chapter, it can move us a long way toward healthy independence. And it allows us to walk toward closeness with our spouse. So does one important final step.

(4) Returning Home by Going Back One More Time

For some, leaving home requires that they return home one more time. For some of us, a stumbling block in our spiritual life can be a lack of forgiveness toward our parents. I took that final step toward "leaving home" when I made a long-distance call from college. Thanks to an outstanding Young Life Leadership program, college had become the period of my most rapid spiritual growth. For the first time, I was digging into God's Word on a consistent basis and learning more about what it would take to be God's man. That's when I ran headlong into a major spiritual roadblock—facing my father and asking his forgiveness.

When my father reestablished contact with my brothers and me, I was beginning high school and had so much anger that I hated him. Then I became a Christian—and I just intensely disliked him! Basically, I kept the same emotions and merely covered them over with a thin Christian veneer.

During that time of intense study of God's Word, I soon recognized the lack of forgiveness toward my father. I remember praying in my dorm room in Texas and asking God to forgive me for all my angry thoughts . . . which I'm sure He did. But I also remember getting up off my knees feeling there was something else I needed to do.

I began flipping through my Bible and suddenly my heart sank. There was a passage of Scripture that I didn't want to read. It laid down too great a challenge. In Matthew 18, I read the story of two debtors. One owed a king a great debt of "ten thousand talents"—close to $10 million in today's terms—and it was time to pay up. Begging for mercy, the man pleaded with the great king, "Have patience with me, and I will repay you everything." In an act of incredible compassion, the king released him from his entire debt and made him a free man!

Without turning to any commentary or Sunday morning message, I knew that debtor was me! When I came to Christ, all my sins had been forgiven. I had a debt so great it could never be paid apart from God's grace and Jesus' shed blood on the cross. There at the cross, He paid my debt in full, releasing me from sin's penalty and its stranglehold on my life. I was free because of what Christ had done.

Then I read the rest of the story. That same slave who had been forgiven so much went out and found one of his fellow slaves who owed him a pittance, just "one hundred denarii." That's less than twenty dollars in today's terms. Yet he "began to choke him, saying, 'Pay back what you owe!'" When word of that exchange got back to the king, he withdrew his mercy and condemned the debtor to jail. Such an ungrateful response after having been forgiven so much incensed the king, who tossed that unforgiving man to the "tormentors."

I sat at my desk, stunned by what I'd read. The conviction was so great I felt as though I'd just received a jolt of electricity throughout my body. Would I forgive my father after receiving forgiveness from my heavenly Father?

I initially tried to explain away my duty. *Yeah, but what about his never being there for me? . . . What about his temper and the times he ridiculed my faith?* I recalled a dozen broken promises and embarrassing displays of anger or worse, and then I counted up the cost. It was a significant sum. *He owed me.* But when I looked, it was a "twenty dollar" debt compared to the "ten million" I'd been forgiven.

I gave up arguing with myself—and with God—and reached for the telephone. It was just a few weeks before I was to go home for spring break, and I had a call to make. My father answered, and agreed to meet me when I came into town. And while I didn't realize it at the time, my intense anger began to drain away with that call. The two weeks went by quickly, and then I drove the eighteen hours straight to Phoenix. The next day, we met for lunch at a local seafood restaurant. We shared shrimp cocktail, fried shrimp, and stuffed shrimp for dessert. (At least we had one thing in common—a liking for shrimp!)

After the meal, I told him how I'd come to know Christ, how *he* could, and that I needed to ask his forgiveness. I'd love to say that what transpired at the table would have been worthy of a Billy Graham movie. You know, the scene where the father and son reconcile after a long season apart. The one where the audience breaks into tears when at the end of the meal the elder man's stubborn pride finally breaks down and he gratefully comes to know Christ. That's the story line I wanted to live out . . . but that's not close to what happened.

In many ways, it was an unremarkable event. I shared from my heart, and he brushed off my testimony and the invitation to come to Christ with hardly a word. When I asked his forgiveness, he said, "Well, if you need that . . ." and then quickly changed the subject. After dinner, we parted with a "See you around." Not a hug nor an "I love you." But somehow, some way, I was different after that one meal. He may not have changed, *but I did*. While the waitress didn't know it, I left something at that table more valuable than any tip. I'd left a truckload of anger, guilt, and shame right there after facing my father.

Don't get me wrong. I didn't talk with him to condone his actions. Sin is sin. Yet my hating him wasn't causing *him* to lose any sleep; it was keeping *me* up at nights.

Leaving home, for some readers (like me), will only come when we take that difficult step in trying to make things right with our parents (or even with their memory). That doesn't mean that if they practice verbal or physical abuse, we have to move back in with them, soaking up emotional left hooks. But to never talk to them simply puts unresolved issues in the deep freeze. The moment a memory is jarred loose or we run into them again, all those old enmities instantly thaw out and we feel a fresh rush of anger and face the temptation of taking it out on a "safer" target than our parents—someone like our spouse or ourselves.

We need to be wise and keep our expectations on Christ if we decide to have a heart-to-heart talk with our parents. Yet even if the meeting isn't all we wanted it to be, it can still have a powerful, positive effect on us. I know. The day I sat down with my father, I felt like I'd taken off a backpack filled with rocks. Amazingly, I even began to feel a level of compassion for him, and later a God-given love for him that I'm sure would not have come otherwise.

These four tips for leaving your first home (including "Facing Family Ghosts" in chapter 8) can mean greater intimacy with your spouse in the home where you now live. All four can be practiced at any time during a marriage. All of them help us in walking toward greater closeness with our spouses and toward a deeper love for all seasons.

CHAPTER 10

Principle #4

CHASING THE
PREDATORS

Sabotage! That's what it had to be, *sabotage*.

U.S. airplanes, desperately needed to fight the Nazi war machine, were grounded during World War II, as their engines were proving defective, again and again. All the evidence pointed to sabotage. The Air Force's Eighth Division had lost as many as forty planes a day in the daylight raids over France. Many more returned to base with one or more engines shot to pieces. The need for engine parts was urgent and rated an A-plus priority. But many replacement parts were being found flawed.

My aunt Dovie had joined thousands of other women like "Rosie the Riveter" and pitched in to do what she could for the war effort. In her case, that meant working double shifts to make replacement aircraft engine parts for the B-17 "Flying Fortresses." Dovie, her coworkers, and her bosses all knew that if the enemy wanted to keep bombers from flying combat missions, one way would be to sabotage desperately needed engine parts. And even though the Nazis were an ocean away from the United States and security was tightened, that's just what was happening! Somehow, a saboteur was loose—and they'd narrowed his or her actions down to Aunt Dovie's department.

My aunt was working in the GM engine division near Indianapolis and was assigned to an assembly line that did the final packing and crating of massive, silver-plated pistons. When the pistons left Building 5, they looked flawless. But after they arrived overseas and were uncrated, the silver plating had countless pin-sized pits and holes that rendered them unsafe and unusable. Intelligence agents backtracked the parts and suspected that some Nazi sympathizer was splashing acid or some other solvent on the pistons before they were crated. But during every shift, and through each step of their manufacture, supervisors, armed security guards, and "G-men" posing as workers watched every step. It had to be someone in the final act of packing, they concluded. Someone Aunt Dovie might have worked alongside day after day! The problem persisted, and the security and spot-checks remained constant. Everyone was suspicious of everyone else.

Then, it happened. One day my aunt walked into the lunchroom and suddenly froze in her tracks. At barely five feet tall and one hundred pounds, my aunt did not look like a spy-killer. But she recognized the enemy. There the spy stood, standing right near the cafeteria entrance. She *knew* it! And soon she made sure her supervisors and everyone else in the plant did as well.

Security personnel quickly captured the traitor, and then smashed it for good measure. "Smashed" it because the traitor was the peanut machine that stood just outside the cafeteria door.

Every day, it had dispensed tasty salted peanuts at just a nickel a handful. Here was the perfect snack to take in your hands and munch on as you walked back to the packing department. And the perfect snack to ruin engine parts. Many of the men and women who had stopped by the peanut machine were failing to wash their hands before picking up and crating the silver pistons. That small amount of salt being transferred from skin to silver plating may have seemed insignificant. Yet, allowed to remain, and given time to do its destructive work, it caused incredible damage.

Who would have thought that something so small could

have caused such a big problem? Though it's only specula-
tion, I think that Solomon's bride would have recognized the
dangers of little things wreaking major havoc.[1] She sure did
during her approaching marriage to Solomon, and she asked
his help to capture "the little foxes" that could undermine
their marriage.

*Couples [need] to take note of problems while they're
small, before they have time to eat away at a couple's
commitment and finally destroy the relationship.*

She saw clearly how "little things," left unchecked or
unnoticed, can lead to unbelievable damage. That's what
we'll see in this fourth way to lasting love. This principle
urges couples to take note of problems while they're small,
before they have time to eat away at a couple's commitment
and finally destroy the relationship. Solomon's bride-to-be
knows they have a "good thing," and she wisely wants to
protect it. That's why, in poetic fashion, she makes a pointed
request of Solomon.

"Catch the foxes for us, the little foxes
that are ruining the vineyards,
while our vineyards are in blossom." (2:15)

"CATCH THE FOXES FOR US..."

Her picture of foxes is clever and appropriate. Foxes were
rampant in Solomon's day, and while they are beautiful animals, farmers knew they were cunning predators capable of
doing much damage. As a shepherdess, the future bride no
doubt had heard stories or seen firsthand what a fox could do.

What an insightful way of picturing the nature of marital
problems! There are some things, such as teasing, telling
only part of the truth to "protect" our spouse, bouncing a
check because we forgot our balance, that when done once
might look "cute," but, left unchecked, actually hold a
predator's power to rip and tear.

The future bride pictures a time of great beauty in their relationship. Everything is in bloom, and her desire is that it stay that way. So she asks him to take the lead in tackling these problems. Notice it's the woman who first spots the potential problems and brings them to the man's attention. Their relationship was one of mutual responsibility and healthy give-and-take. Here, she uses her God-given protective instincts to alert him of potential problems and then calls on him to use his God-given "hunting" instincts to track them down! Men, the next time your wife points out an issue in your relationship, don't resent it as an intrusion, but welcome it as wise counsel.

What Solomon's future bride says parallels the wisdom found in an insightful proverb.

> "I passed by the field of the sluggard
> And by the vineyard of the man lacking sense,
> And behold, it was completely overgrown with thistles;
> Its surface was covered with nettles,
> And its stone wall was broken down.
> When I saw, I reflected upon it;
> I looked, and received instructions.
> 'A little sleep, a little slumber,
> A little folding of the hands to rest,'
> Then your poverty will come as a robber,
> And your want like an armed man." (24:30–34)

The above verses could be the "expanded version" of her words in Song of Songs. In this case, it's a sluggard who has let his vineyard go. It's in a terrible state of disrepair, and instead of being beautiful, its blossoms have been choked out by thistles and nettles. Its walls are crumbling, allowing easy access to any wild animal or wayfarer, and it comes with a chilling prediction. For those who "fold their hands" and don't keep up with the everyday maintenance necessary, one day they'll be confronted by a merciless robber who strips them of everything of value.

There is so much wisdom in the words of Solomon's

bride. She draws a protective picture of love for all of us who would guard his or her home. Yet, we must admit that it's a challenge to deal with issues at the "fox" level, before they turn into a ravaging "lions." For one thing, they seem like annoyances, not fundamental issues. "Small" things like bouncing a check, procrastinating on a chore, skipping church to sleep in on Sunday, or sniping at each other. Yet these "little foxes" can quickly grow into patterns of behavior or personal problems that become irritants and then genuine threats to the health and stability of our relationship. How can we deal with these issues while they're still at the "fox" level?

If you want to increase the love level in your marriage, you will follow this fourth way to intimacy, chasing away the predators that nip at your relationship. Here are six common issues that often get listed in the "minor" category; yet like a "fox" in a sheep pen, if ignored or underestimated for any length of time, each can cause great havoc. Then we'll look at a proven, six-part plan for taking these problems captive and chasing them away from our lives.

HOW TO LET LITTLE FOXES
BECOME STRONG PREDATORS

1. Turn Past Issues into Emotional Earthquakes

Growing up, Phil watched his mother recklessly spend every dime that came her way. As a single mother, she put great strain on the rest of the family with her spending binges; at times even the basics were unavailable. When his mother died, Phil and the rest of the family still weren't free from her "spending" problem. Unknown to them, she had run up a great deal of credit card debt that the family was forced to pay.

That was a *past* issue, but he's still fighting it today. If Phil's wife, Diane, goes over budget on an item they've discussed, even if it's only by a few dollars and for a good reason, Phil lets loose with an earthquake of emotions. Diane's minor overage should have recorded a 1.7 on the emotional "Richter" scale, but Phil responds with a 7.1 quake! That's because he isn't reacting to a present problem alone; he's responding to the past. In effect, he's yelling at his mother as much as he's shouting at Diane. Phil must address his past, or it will cripple his present relationship with his wife.

It doesn't have to be issues with family either. For instance, if a woman works with an angry boss day after day, she can develop a hypersensitivity to any criticism her husband utters. It's as though she has developed a long-term "relational sunburn," caused by her past exposure to cutting words. As a result, she interprets any constructive correction her husband gives as gross insensitivity. Unresolved problems with other people can creep into our marriage and act like a fox.

2. Add Physical Distance When You Communicate

Think about a recent argument you've had with your spouse. Did you begin by sitting across the room or talking to each other from opposite sides of the island kitchen? When you're talking with your spouse, the physical distance you maintain between one another is often a good indication of the emotional distance in the relationship. Studies show that meaningful communication *decreases* as the distance between spouses increases.

It's a small thing to sit next to our spouse. It's also a small thing to begin letting physical distance push its way into our way of relating. If it's been a few years since you've actually sat next to your spouse in the car—shock the kids and buckle in the middle seat like you did when you were dating! Instead of sitting in your favorite chair in front of the TV, go and snuggle up to your wife on the love seat. Take a hard look at the "comfortable distance" you two have developed— Has it spread out so far that it's a fox on its way to becoming a lion?

3. Listen Little

Some spouses don't really listen. They tell themselves, *Why should I bother to listen? I know what he (or she) is going to say anyway.* So their spouse is struggling to express an important idea and, knowing already what he or she is trying to say, they finish the idea.

In almost every marriage, one partner is "quicker to the draw" when it comes to framing verbal messages. A real act of love is to listen attentively to your spouse and patiently wait for him or her to finish speaking. The book of Proverbs puts it in much stronger terms. "He who gives an answer before he hears, it is folly and shame to him" (18:13).

None of us has a crystal ball when it comes to communication. Even though we may be certain that the current thought our spouse is expressing is one we've heard 8,000 times before, we need to give our mate the gift of uninterrupted conversation. Even if the same old thing is being said, there may be a reason for it. Perhaps your spouse never felt heard the previous 7,999 times! Listen lightly, and you will miss valuable information. Listen intently, and you will hear the truth.

4. Avoid Talking About the Hard Issues

Justin struggled with the thought of "hurting" his wife. That's why he was so careful to be indirect when it came to talking about their finances or what was happening in his job. His wife never could get a straight answer from him about where they stood—until the couch she had been sitting on was repossessed by a bill collector!

It's true, some subjects are hard to talk about. Additionally, a spouse doesn't need to know of every little struggle or minor slight we experience. But hiding *major* personal or financial issues from a loved one is an invitation to disaster. If we can't be open, vulnerable, and honest with our spouse, we're letting foxes run loose in our relationship.

5. Don't Worry About Your Tone of Voice

In a scene from the Academy Award-winning movie *Patton*, the army general is incensed because his troops have fought to a standstill in the rugged mountains of Italy. With fury in his voice, he thunders at his commanders, "We don't stop. *We advance.* You have twenty-four hours to make a breakthrough. If you can't get the job done, *I'll fire you and get someone who can!*" After his commanders leave to go back to the front lines, a trusted aide approaches Patton and says,

"General, you shouldn't talk that way. The men don't know when you're kidding."

"That doesn't matter," Patton replies. "It only matters if *I* know."

That kind of thinking is dangerous, for if we say one thing with our tone of voice but mean another, our loved one can be confused. In fact, we have *miscommunicated*. An incorrect tone of voice is a dangerous little fox.

An angry tone of voice is one such "fox" that can quickly turn into a predator. Much of the anger expressed by husbands and wives is, like Patton's outburst, dramatic acting for effect. "*This time*, they're getting the message loud and clear," we tell ourselves. But instead of calmly re-explaining a point, we turn up the volume level ten notches. (We know our words are getting through, because their hair is being blow-dried while we talk to them!)

Once you begin yelling or acting out in anger, you're off the issue being discussed. Now you've let a protective wall crumble, and the foxes are in the vineyard. When that happens, there's a related problem with having anger loose in your relationship as well.

Though words are important, listeners cannot ignore your tone of voice. Speak with love, patience, and self-control. Anger, sarcasm, and indifference in your voice can unleash pesky foxes in your marriage. Be sure your tone of voice and your accompanying facial expressions enhance your words rather than contradict them.[2]

6. Downplay Your Words

We all know the nursery rhyme "Sticks and stones can break my bones, but words can never hurt me." We all know it's a lie. Words can devastate a spouse and destroy a marriage. Many of my counselees tell me that words spoken by their spouse in anger have hurt them for years. For some people, they can close their eyes and still see their *parents'* angry eyes and dramatic gestures of decades ago.

As important as tone of voice is, we cannot ignore our actual words. Words count much and are not quickly forgotten. Good words can heal, but bad words can destroy a person's spirit. We may tell our lover, "I didn't really mean it. I apologize." The other person may accept our apology, yet wonder if we truly meant what we said.

Words of love and caring never have to be apologized for. Yet angry words spoken in the heat of battle can smash the life out of a marriage. Proverbs puts it this way, "A soothing tongue is a tree of life, but perversion in it crushes the spirit" (15:4). We're kidding ourselves if we think that angry words don't have a potential to crush our spouse.

We've observed the many little foxes in marriage that can turn into major predators in a hurry. What's a couple to do to protect themselves? First, take the first three ways of lasting love (chapters 3–9) and apply them fully in your relationship. Then I recommend a proven problem-solving method that can be used to attack concerns at the "fox" level—or to help shrink "lion-sized" issues down to manageable size.

FOX HUNTING

Here is a proven plan for avoiding or reducing problems. To hunt down and capture those loose foxes before they become major problems, I recommend the following six steps.

1. Recognize the Need to Do Some Things Differently

Zach and Diane had an unhealthy motto they lived by: "If it doesn't work . . . *keep doing it.*" Though they didn't have that motto nailed on a kitchen wall, they lived it out by their actions. Diane had gotten down on herself after their third child was born. She had gone through the normal postpartum mood swings, and the significant amount of weight gained from the pregnancy wasn't coming off like before, making her feel even more depressed.

Zach had the best of intentions when he told her, "Honey, you can lose that weight, I know you can!" But he did not simply listen to Diane's frustrations; instead, he gave her pep talks. When she didn't seem to respond, Zach redoubled his efforts, paying for a membership in a health club for her and lecturing her on the dangers to her and the kids of her pessimism. When she still didn't respond, he urged her to "pray about her negative attitude," bought her a shelf full of health store vitamins, and insisted that she go to the doctor for a physical checkup.

More of the same doesn't bring change.

Nothing worked. In fact, very soon, the solution he was trying so hard to force on his wife was actually a major part of the problem! He loved her too much to just watch her "become fat and unhappy," but he wasn't willing to realize that what he was doing daily wasn't helping bring any change. He needed to do more of something different—not more of the same. He could have become more vulnerable himself—drawing out her nurturing side—or acknowledged her feelings or asked her what she felt might help (or a number of other things). Instead, he did "more of the same" even though it brought fewer results.

Without exaggeration, I cannot think of a counseling session when I haven't said to an individual or couple who felt "stuck" in a problem, "More of the same doesn't bring change." So if a "single shot" solution won't work, what will? We begin by recognizing our strengths in the relationship.

2. Focus on Your Strengths

When the church at Ephesus had gotten off track, the resurrected Lord Jesus Himself told believers there, "I know your deeds and your toil and perseverance . . ." and named a number of other positive qualities (Revelation 2:1–5). "But I have this against you, that you have left your first love."

The remedy for a dwindling love, the Lord Jesus said, was to first look at what they'd done right. "Remember," He says, "from where you've fallen." In other words, they needed to remember the times they were "on top of things," serving Him with their whole hearts and walking closely with their Savior. The same principle is extremely important for married couples to apply who would see their love light stay bright and shining. If you're facing a problem today, take time together to look at your relationship strengths. As you look at your relationship (even going back to your courtship if you have to), what have you done well as a couple? Were there times when you've been sensitive to each other's needs? Have there been times when you've worked through a problem or made a decision together where both of you walked away feeling closer than before?

Couples who are struggling "today," often are husbands and wives who have forgotten that "back a few miles" in their journey were successes and genuine strengths. Going back to times in your relationship where things worked well, even if those periods were only a short period of time, can give you an important platform to face current issues today.

3. State a Clear Goal

Time and again, I'll ask a couple who seems stuck, "Where would you like to be in your relationship?" Most of the time, they are experts at attacking each other and telling me what's wrong with their relationship. But they stop and stumble when you ask them what their *goals* are as a couple.

You begin to move past a problem when you clearly express a goal. Goal setting is a serious and important part of dealing with problems. It doesn't trivialize a problem to break it down into concrete, action-oriented steps. It's helpful! Notice that in His advice to the Ephesus church in Revelation 2, the Lord tells the Ephesian believers to do three things to rekindle their love for Him: "Remember from where you have fallen, repent and do the things you did at first" (v. 5). To "repent" means to "turn around" and begin walking toward God's best. And to "do the things you did at first" is a call to get with a program that's brought success. Call them steps, principles, pictures, or points—just do them!

How does this actually work in real life? First, come up with a written "goal" for dealing with an issue. For example, a husband is very frustrated with his wife, who often "breaks their budget" by buying something unexpected; he is frustrated even if she buys when the item is on sale. Spending differences can certainly be "foxes" that turn into "lions." To head off the problem while it's still small (or make it smaller if it's already roaring out of control), they first set a goal. They come up with a written goal: "Neither of us can spend more than $50.00 that isn't budgeted for without calling the other person first." That stops the rationalization "It's easier to ask forgiveness than permission!" and it gives them a specific goal that, if needed, can even be broken down into specific steps.

Clear goals take a negative problem and start you on the way to constructive change.

4. Divide the Goal into Measurable Behaviors

Carl and Heather face a "fox" of their own: Heather doesn't feel listened to. Together, they agree to look at the problem, break it down, and propose specific actions for a solution. They express that solution as a multipart goal. Such steps help husbands and wives answer a powerful question, "How will you know when things are better in this area?" It's amazing how some couples can make legitimate, even significant changes, but somehow miss or discount them because no standard has been set!

Couples can capture "little foxes" if they'll take their concern, set a goal, and then break it into concrete steps. Carl and Heather, for example, developed three specific steps:

1. When he walks in the door, he'll spend the first ten minutes talking to me before going over to watch the news.

2. I'll know he's listening when he asks me two follow-up questions after I've shared something important. (A follow-up question would be something like, "Then how did that make you feel?" or "What do you think that means?")

3. He will have a videotape in the VCR, when he's watching a football game (ready to record the action), so that, if I do ask him a question, he can look at me and give me his full attention instead of looking around me at the television.

With these steps, Carl knew specific things to do, and Heather could measure progress in the problem area. Reaching the goal by setting up concrete steps not only gives a man the ability to aim his "hunter instinct" at specific problems, but it helps the wife crystallize what she really wants to be different in the relationship. This leads to step five in hunting for problem foxes.

5. When Minor Improvements Occur, Have a Party

When the Prodigal Son returned, there wasn't anything halfway about his reception back home (Luke 15:20–24). I'm not suggesting throwing a party the first time your husband puts a tape in the VCR during a game so you can "talk" during the fourth quarter, or the first time your wife calls you at work to say, "Honey, there's something on sale for over $50.00 that we really need. What do you think?" But celebration certainly is appropriate.

At the least, give your spouse a hug, a word of praise or appreciation, or even put your list on the refrigerator. Borrow a gold star from the kids' sticker book, and give him or her a star! (Remember how motivating that was in grade school or Sunday school?)

Such an honest celebration isn't something that trivializes what has happened but reinforces it. Skip the "gold star" if you think it's too juvenile, but don't skip praising your spouse when he or she makes a legitimate step toward positive change. By doing so, you're not doing "more of the same" but something that can help make your marriage "foxproof." Finally:

6. Stay Open to Change Through All Seasons

One final step in keeping the fences up and the foxes out is to try different activities to keep your relationship strong and healthy. Come up with your own list of things that "color outside the lines." Here are a few ideas:

- *If it's been a while since the two of you went out to breakfast, schedule a breakfast date.*

- *If you haven't seen a movie in two years, start watching for something redeeming to see together.*

- *If you've never gone on a weekend "missions" outreach, sign up!*

- *If you've never been on a three-day Christian cruise, start saving up for one.*

- *If your church has a Saturday evening service you haven't yet attended, make it your church service that week.*

Being open to new things is important in solving problems and keeping your love strong. One of the greatest examples of someone who continues to find vitality and new life in his ministry and marriage is my friend and fellow author Chuck Swindoll. When Cindy and I were at a booksellers' banquet a few years ago, Chuck and his wife, Cynthia, greeted us. With twinkling eyes, he told me, "Trent, just say 'yes' to what I'm about to ask you."

"What's that?" I asked.

"I want you and Cindy to join Cynthia and me on a motorcycle trip. We're taking our Harley and going from Portland all the way down the coast to L.A. It's going to be great! *You guys gotta come!*"

Not having the days available or our own Harley, we couldn't join them on their motorcycle trip. But Cindy and I are committed to building in times of refreshment in our marriage. (In chapter 14 I recommend a "weekend of change" as part of the final way to intimacy, "Planned Spontaneity.")

My prayer for you, dear reader, is that you'll act purposefully and persistently to catch those "little foxes" that come with any relationship.

CHAPTER 11

Principle #5
ENJOYING
PHYSICAL INTIMACY

Growing up in a single-parent home, each of us three boys took on chores around the house at an early age. Then at an earlier age than any of our friends, we all added "odd jobs" to earn a little extra money to contribute to the family kitty. That's why, at age eight, I took on the mighty responsibility of walking a "donut route." Such "routes" were very popular back in the 1950s, but they disappeared almost entirely by the 1960s—and I think I was a large factor in their demise.

On a "donut route," the local bakery truck would pull up to an appointed spot, and the driver would hand out huge wire-mesh baskets filled with sacks of donuts to several waiting boys. (There were ten of us.) Picture it as a Dunkin' Donuts delivery service. Only instead of people calling in orders, the delivery "men" were boys without any definite orders who walked down streets with baskets full of donuts. I especially liked knocking on doors and hearing people say, "Oh, I shouldn't . . ." and then take four dozen chocolate.

One afternoon I had visited perhaps a dozen houses and already half my donuts were gone. I knocked on the next door and a nice lady answered the door. This was well before hand-held mixers were common, and she was wearing an apron, stirring a big bowl of cake batter with a large wooden spoon.

"Would you like some donuts, ma'am?" I asked. "They're really fresh—just came from the bakery. I know you'd like them," I said, having put my basket down and holding out two sacks of jellies in one hand and a sack of glazed in the other. Just the smell could have made the most disciplined dieter's willpower shatter on the spot. It was so easy to sell them, I'm sure the government found out about it and declared it illegal.

"Oh, I shouldn't . . . ," she said, looking right at the jellies. "Well, I guess I could take just one . . . make that *two* dozen of the jellies." She pushed open the door and took both sacks of the jellies and then asked, "Would you mind stirring my cake batter while I go in and get the money?"

"No, ma'am," I said. "I can do that." One of my chores around the house was helping to cook, so I gladly obliged her while she went in to get the donut money. Just when she came back, the phone rang. "Keep stirring, honey!" she said, and then she disappeared again to get the phone.

All this time, I'd been blowing bubbles with my Bazooka bubble gum. As I stirred and blew bubbles, I blew one bubble so large it could have easily qualified for the Cooperstown "Hall of Famous Bubbles." Not wanting to burst it, I held the large bowl tightly with my left hand and arm and reached for the weather balloon-sized bubble with my right.

As I stared at the incredible size of the still inflated bubble, the door banged open and the lady reappeared. Unfortunately, the door startled me, and I dropped the bubble gum right into the cake batter! I stood there in shock as the lady scooped the bowl from my hands, handed me the money for donuts, and began whipping the mix. The bubble gum disappeared! And in a flash, she disappeared behind a closed door with a "Thanks, sugar. Bye."

I stood on the doorstep a long time, debating whether I should knock on the door and tell her what had happened. But it was getting late, and I couldn't figure out how I'd explain it to her . . . so I finished my route and walked home. That night, I remember sitting at the dinner table and, at a quiet point during the meal, innocently asking my mother,

"Mom? What happens when you bake bubble gum in a cake?"

A great unsolved mystery to me has always been what that extra "ingredient" did to that poor woman's cake. (I can just hear her husband saying, "Honey, the cake sure is chewy tonight!")

If you're wondering what bubble gum in the cake mix has to do with a chapter on sexual intimacy, the answer is, "Quite a lot!" When it comes to sexual intimacy—and cake making—lasting success comes only by adding the right ingredients.

We live in a society that mixes in misinformation about sex every opportunity it gets. Whether it's books like *Men Are Just Desserts* or *Nice Girls Do and So Should You,* or the unrealistic and exaggerated physical descriptions of sex in movies and on television, many ideas about sexual intimacy before and during marriage are only half-baked ideas unfit for human consumption. What's a person to do? If you want a Betty Crocker cake mix to come out right, then you need to follow the directions printed on the label, using the exact ingredients. If you want to have a sexual relationship as beautiful as your wedding cake, then get your baking instructions from the Author of intimacy Himself. Right here in the Song of Songs is every ingredient you need to have an exciting, fulfilling sexual relationship. And in Song 4:12–15 we now find a key ingredient in the fifth principle for a love for a lifetime: the God-ordained enjoyment of sexual intimacy. Yes, marvelous marital sex is something God heartily endorses, beginning with a couple's wedding night.

IN THE MARRIAGE GARDEN

In earlier chapters, we've seen the great lengths Solomon goes to make their first night of physical union a wonderful experience. He praises his bride seven times before he touches her, and then calls on her to "leave" her home and "cleave" to him. Now after a time of verbal praise on their wedding night, they begin a time of physical enjoyment.

In an honoring way, the Scriptures continue to walk us

through this special evening of romance. In Song 4:9, Solomon's excitement is obvious. He says to her, "You have made my heart beat faster, my sister, my bride; you have made my heart beat faster with a single glance of your eyes." With his heart beating like a freight train, they then partake in passionate kissing as Solomon declares, "Your lips, my bride, drip honey; honey and milk are under your tongue" (v. 11).

One more time Solomon praises her in verses 12–15; he uses the metaphor of a private garden and its fruits. The couple are about to enter into intercourse, and he praises her again, this time for keeping herself pure for their wedding night. He says of her, "A garden locked is my sister, my bride. A rock garden locked, a spring sealed up."[1]

After all this preparation, his bride is only too ready to respond. In fact, she invites him to join her with the words:

> "Awake, O north wind,
> And come, wind of the south;
> Make my garden breathe out fragrance,
> Let its spices be wafted abroad.
> May my beloved come into his garden
> And eat its choice fruits!" (4:16)

At this point as they move toward each other, the time of preparation is over, and the curtain closes on our two lovers. The description sensitively stops here as two of God's own enjoy privately one of God's good gifts—the sexual act of marriage. Later, it's Solomon who breaks the spell and speaks again, describing in a poetic way how fully and completely they enjoyed their lovemaking.

> "I have come into my garden, my sister, my bride;
> I have gathered my myrrh along with my balsam.
> I have eaten my honeycomb and my honey;
> I have drunk my wine and my milk." (5:1a)

What a descriptive way of picturing a fulfilling experience. And then comes a pronouncement of blessing: "Eat, friends;

drink and imbibe deeply, O lovers" (5:1b). Announcing His approval is the One who invented human physical responsiveness and was there the whole time—God Himself. As one Bible commentator writes:

> In the final analysis this must be the voice of the Creator, the greatest Poet, the most intimate wedding guest of all. The One who indeed prepared this lovely couple for the night of His design. He lifts His voice and gives hearty approval to the entire night. He vigorously endorses and affirms the love of this couple. He takes pleasure in what has taken place. Two of His own have experienced love in all the beauty and fervor and purity that He intended for them.[2]

What a platform this couple had to launch an evening of intimacy! And what a challenge for us to do the same. But do Solomon and his bride represent an ideal of intimacy that none of us can ever hope to attain? The answer is, "Yes" and "No." Yes, they are a picture of God's best; and no, their experience isn't reserved just for kings and queens. It is something God designed for all His "saints" who are invited to "eat, friends; drink and imbibe deeply, O lovers!"

> *There's never been a better time than right now to raise your level of sexual intimacy.*

Let me give you a challenge. *There's never been a better time than right now to raise your level of sexual intimacy.* But how? First, avoid three common misconceptions about sex that can drain away physical desire and responsiveness. Then follow six practical ways to nurture marital intimacy.

THREE COMMON MISCONCEPTIONS TO AVOID
1. Pornography Is Healthy Stimulation
The truth is, pornography is sinful and has dramatic consequences. I remember watching a pastor and seminary pro-

fessor from a so-called conservative seminary tell a talk show host about ways to "rev up your sexual motors." But he didn't share anything you'll find in this chapter. Rather, right on national TV he explained what he thought was perfectly appropriate preparation for sex—pornography.

The host loved it, and the audience roared when this professor told an incredible story. "I've been married so long," he said, "frankly, it can get boring making love to the same woman. So what my wife and I have agreed to do is something I recommend for everyone. I get a *Playboy* or *Penthouse* magazine centerfold and lay it on the pillow next to me. That way, by looking at that picture, I'm making it more interesting to me, and find I 'perform' better for her."

I nearly fell on the floor when I heard that! Here was a Christian, actively looking at pornography *while* he made love to his wife? One could quickly think of a dozen verses that would condemn such a practice as out-and-out sin.[3]

Don't buy the world's nodding approval that pornography, whether in movies or magazines, *aids* in increasing genuine intimacy. It doesn't. It may bring excitement for a moment, but like all sin, the pleasure only lasts for a season. Pornography has a fast-fading effect that demands more and more, and wilder and wilder, to reach the same level of excitement. Then at its worst, it can lock a person fast into an incredibly damaging addiction.

Pornography, by its basic nature, teaches that stimulation comes from "outside" a person. It uses every trick of the camera to make sexual intimacy into exploiting marathons that real life people can't win. Solomon and his bride have already taught us that lasting excitement comes *from within*. In a healthy marriage, it's their relationship, not just their physical appearance, that makes lovemaking so special.

2. *Turning Your Marriage into an "Affair" Protects It*

The truth is, treating your marriage as though it were an affair attacks the marriage. Yet one couple I counseled were considering the advice of a popular book that urged couples to "treat their marriage like an affair." That worldly advice is *terrible* counsel. Affairs are brief, turbulent, erratic fits of emotion outside of God's blessing and will. Pretending your spouse is a secret lover may increase the excitement level in the short run (so too does playing Russian roulette)—but it's an excitement that can't be sustained in real life. Such a fantasy relationship sows only more seeds of discontentment.

If you're looking for lasting excitement, that comes from God's plan. Sex for the Christian has every advantage to make it outstanding. It adds the elements of trust and acceptance from committing ourselves to our "best friend" and life partner. And it's where fulfillment, freedom from guilt, and God's blessing all reside.

3. Frequent and Exotic Sexual Performance Sustains a Marriage

The truth is, seeking after sexual performance can bring performance anxiety and unnecessary challenges. I suspect that most of us struggle to be "average." For example, if we make "less than the average" salary, or spend more on groceries than the "average" family, we wonder where we've gone wrong! Unfortunately, many couples also struggle to keep up with what they believe is "average" in the area of sex. They're more concerned with reading reports about what the "average" American's sex life is like than they are with enjoying the physical aspects of their own marriage.

> *Trying to keep on par with national averages will not produce sexual satisfaction. In fact, it's almost guaranteed to produce just the opposite effect. . . .*

Often those reports translate into goals for frequency and variety of sexual performance. How should couples interpret the figures supplied in such reports as Masters and Johnson and other sex researchers? *Frankly, I recommend you don't look at them at all.* Trying to keep on par with national averages will not produce sexual satisfaction. In fact, it's almost guaranteed to produce just the opposite effect by introducing performance anxiety.

In day-to-day life, there will be periods of high sexual activity and periods when little activity takes place. If a couple wants to look for the right "level" of sexual involvement, I suggest they turn to Scripture for its simple, freeing counsel:

> The husband must fulfill his duty to his wife, and likewise also the wife to her husband. The wife does not have authority over her own body, but the husband does; and likewise also the husband does not have authority over his own body, but the wife does. (1 Corinthians 7:3–5)

In other words, a desire to respond to one another in love and to meet one another's needs is the best guideline in deciding how and when to be physically intimate. Chasing a national average is a barrier, not a breakthrough, to a healthy sexual relationship. While a regular pattern of sexual contact is desirable, no tables or charts need dictate a loving couple's actions. With those cautions in mind, let's look at several ways to nurture sexual intimacy in marriage.

SIX WAYS TO NOURISH
A POSITIVE SEXUAL RESPONSE

1. Understand What Does and Doesn't Come Naturally

"We used to really enjoy being intimate," Denise said. "But over the years, it seems like what was once so natural just doesn't work."

Enjoying intimacy isn't always a matter of "doing what comes naturally." In fact, what may be natural to us (if we came from a damaged or non-Christian background) may be even counterproductive when it comes to increasing intimacy! For example, I counseled a couple who were new Christians, where he had been married four times and this was her third marriage. "Doing what came naturally" in their seven combined marriages nearly ended this marriage, so ignorant were they of basic sexual physiology and God-honoring advice.

Every man and woman has the physical potential to enjoy and give enjoyment in the sexual area, unless there are primary organic problems. Yet the "natural" act of sexual intimacy can become forced or even "unnatural." I ask couples who feel like they're "stuck" with a lower level of intimacy than they'd like to study the following chart. Although most couples have a high degree of excitement at the beginning of their marriage, when one or more of these various "layers of life" become blocked or clogged, you can expect to experience a draining effect when it comes to the desire for or enjoyment of sex. Just look below at how many factors can influence—positively or negatively—the sexual act. Let's consider each of these eight areas in detail.

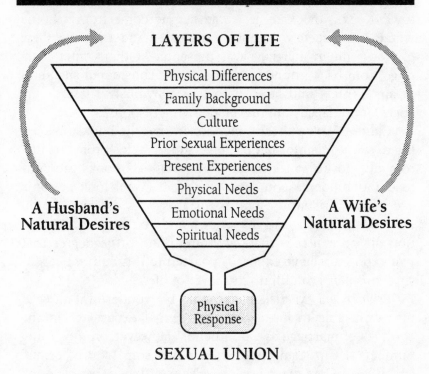

AREAS THAT AFFECT OUR SEXUAL RELATIONSHIP

LAYERS OF LIFE

Physical Differences

Family Background

Culture

Prior Sexual Experiences

Present Experiences

Physical Needs

Emotional Needs

Spiritual Needs

A Husband's Natural Desires

A Wife's Natural Desires

Physical Response

SEXUAL UNION

Physical differences. I can't stress enough how important it is for every couple—from the doctors and nurses I've worked with to that couple with seven previous marriages—to understand basic physiological functioning. Often, spouses simply are unaware of how powerfully physical differences can affect the quality of their involvement. For example, conservative estimates from sex researchers note that when it comes to sexual readiness and arousal, a husband can become fully aroused in *ninety seconds*, whereas a wife can take between fifteen and *thirty minutes*. Just understanding that one physical difference and adding time to prepare each person can make lovemaking more fulfilling.

Family background. Unfortunately, studies show that few people learn about sex directly from their parents, yet individuals are still greatly influenced by their families' attitudes toward sex. For example, some people come from a home where sexual facts were openly discussed and a positive view of God's gift in marriage was presented. Others enter marriage from backgrounds where sex was considered shameful in any context and laced with fear. Obviously, these differences, if not faced, can prevent a loving response.

Culture. We've already mentioned that the bookstores are filled with misinformation on "super" sex. From steamy romance novels to technical sex reports, sex books can confuse and hinder a couple's sexual life. (We'll look at some excellent Christian resources in this area later.) Add in movies, television, and magazines, and you've got a description of "normal" sex that's anything but. To the degree that you expose (or have exposed) yourself to this cultural confusion, problems can fill up this layer of life.

Prior sexual experiences. It would be wonderful if all couples were able to have their first sexual experience in the confines of marriage as God intends. However, an increasing number of Christian couples have had some sort of sexual encounter before marriage. As we've mentioned, people don't easily forget the feelings of guilt, regret, and remorse that result from premarital sexual activity (or tragically, incest or rape). If left unforgiven and unconfronted, it can create "emotional scar tissue" that can block a person from fully enjoying marital sex.

Present experiences. We also are strongly affected by the present. A "hard day at the office" or a "rough time with the kids" can significantly reduce a person's capacity to feel caring or loving toward a spouse.

Physical and emotional needs. Certain needs can act like a sponge in soaking up sexual desire. A long-term illness or other physical or emotional problem can severely diminish sexual desire.

Spiritual needs. Problems in this area can be the most destructive of all. If our relationship is not right with the Lord, we can expect other areas of life to be out of balance too. Spiritual intimacy between a couple connects them at the very deepest level with the Lord and with each other. Couples who lose their desire to pray or spend time with the Lord often lose their sexual desire for one another as well. That's because as they move away from the God who brought them together, they're walking away from Him who holds them together as well.

The spiritual commitment will affect their enjoyment of and involvement in sex. Perhaps that's why one University of Chicago study based on a survey of thousands of women reported that religious women were more satisfied with the frequency of intercourse and felt freer to discuss sex more openly with their husbands than nonreligious women.[4]

Each of these "layers of life" can affect a husband's or wife's sexual desire. How well we respond to each other is often a product of how clear or cluttered these various "layers" are. How can you keep each area clear and unclogged? Begin by creative caring.

2. Focus on Creative Caring and Communication

It's a fact that "small, specific, positive, caring actions" distinguish clinically unstable couples from close-knit ones.[5] Close-knit couples still do small loving acts on a consistent basis. Things like calling from work to say "Hello" and "I love you," writing a note, or giving their spouse a five-minute back rub (no strings attached!). The husbands still are willing to open doors for their wives, even though they have been married for years.

Let me encourage you and your spouse to prepare your own Caring List. Each of you write down on a piece of paper ten small, specific, positive things that your wife (or husband) could do for you that would say, "You're important to me. I appreciate you." Small things like those in the Caring List below.

Sample Caring List

Husband's List	Wife's List
1. Put out the sports page for me	1. Call me from work
2. Give me a five-minute back rub	2. Bathe the kids for me
3. Watch one quarter of a game with me	3. Write me a note
4. Hug me when I get home	4. Hold my hand when we're walking
5. Ask me what happened at work that was interesting	5. Ask me three "follow-up questions" about my day
6. Take an evening walk with me	6. Stay at the table until I'm finished
7. Put on a CD I like in the evening	7. Put your dirty clothes in the hamper
8. Tell me you prayed for me today	8. Ask me about the children's needs
9. Take time to "calendar" our schedule	9. Rent and watch a movie with me
10. Compliment me on the yard	10. Bring me a Snickers candy bar

---

Once you have your list, exchange it with your spouse. Then the two of you commit to picking one thing (out of the ten) on each other's list to do each day, Monday through Friday (skip the weekends!). In the course of an average month, that's twenty small, specific, positive things you've done to say "I love you" that you know are making an investment in your spouse's account.

While all these small, loving actions may seem to be unrelated to sexual intimacy, they're not. My friend Kevin Lehman had it right with the title of his book, *Sex Begins in the Kitchen*. He didn't mean that you grab your spouse in the midst of doing the dishes, but that doing the dishes is the best way to have your spouse grab you in a more romantic time and place.

Caring acts are important for increasing intimacy. So too is another wise choice that begins with a question.

3. Be Willing to Ask Questions

Remember the couple with seven marriages between them? In addition, they had had a host of sexual partners in between in their days before Christ. Yet all that physical history was just *reinforcing* sexual problems, not solving them. Like I do with all the premarital couples I see, I had them listen to Dr. Ed Wheat's wonderful cassette tapes for married couples called "Intended for Pleasure." The day this couple came back in for counseling after listening to these tapes, he broke down and cried in my office. Here sat a fifty-five-year-old man with loads of sexual experience, and yet he knew so little of male/female response that he was ashamed to hold up his head.

He may have felt foolish for asking so many basic questions, but he shouldn't have. It is crucial that couples get the right answers to their questions on sexual response and even intimacy problems from a godly source. While there is an increasing number of books on Christian bookshelves that can help, two author teams I recommend are Ed and Gayle Wheat and Clifford and Joyce Penner. In a sensitive yet specific way, they offer accurate answers to many commonly asked questions.[6]

Be wise enough to ask questions. When you do, you're joining a select group of folks interested in wise counsel. They're people who understand the truth presented in Proverbs, "Only the wise seek counsel," and "Fools despise wisdom and instruction."

4. Understand That Rest Is a Sexual Stimulant

Do you want to increase your degree of sexual intimacy—overnight? Then I recommend you understand an almost universally overlooked fact; namely, nighttime often isn't the best time for sex. Now, it *can* be, if both people are rested and relaxed and the house is quiet. But for most couples, they're so exhausted by the end of a long day at work and with kids that intimacy is dismissed with "too much trouble" or "I'm just too tired."

Did you know that in terms of sexual hormones, they are at their *peak* with most people when they wake up? As an experiment, why not lock your bedroom door before you go to sleep and set the alarm clock early to enjoy a time of intimacy when you're more rested and relaxed? Whether it's picking a "less stressed" time or just lowering the level of stress in our lives, both can add greatly to sexual intimacy.

5. Find Fulfillment in Touching and Pleasure

Some couples fall into the trap that intimacy solely equals the act of intercourse. They discount kissing or petting or simply lying next to each other in an intimate way. What a mistake! "Pleasuring"—the sexual feelings from touch and physical closeness—can be fulfilling apart from intercourse.

Solomon and his bride enjoyed just being together, praising each other, looking into each other's eyes, kissing, and caressing. If a spouse only feels that she's being reached for for "one thing," it can bring a hesitant or rejecting response —not a willingness to let the other person near. Like we saw on Solomon's wedding night, enjoy the whole "feast" of physical interaction that God endorses.

6. Turn Your Lovemaking Over to the Lord

Finally, couples can certainly pray about their lovemaking, asking God to make that time of intimacy all He designed it to be. But there's a natural increase in the platform for intimacy just in knowing and growing in Christ! Take a moment to think of just a few of the many advantages you gain as a growing believer. There's freedom from guilt, anger, and bitterness that comes when we confess our sins to God and ask our spouse for forgiveness when we've wronged him or her. This absence of guilt and anger brings a wonderful inner freedom that enhances our desire to embrace our loved one.

Also, there's a marked decrease in *fear* for those who know and love Jesus. In 1 John 4:18, we're told that "Perfect love casts out fear." Unfortunately, the opposite is true as well. The more fear we have in our lives, the less loving we're going to be as a person. In other words, as God's "perfect" love fills our life, the net result is that we become more loving people—including more lovable and approachable with our spouse! And that is a key way to nurture intimacy in marriage.

CHAPTER 12

Principle #6

LEADERSHIP THAT DRAWS TWO TOGETHER

My colleague Gary Smalley and I had just finished leading a family seminar held on the beautiful island of Kodiak, Alaska, and decided to wrap things up by fishing for king salmon. Fishing in Alaska during their nearly twenty-four hours of summer daylight is a dream come true. The only thing that keeps your line out of the water is when you drive back to town for food and a few hours of sleep. Then you're right back to fighting bigger fish than the ones hanging in Red Lobster! It was food and rest that brought Gary's oldest son, Greg, and me back into town and into a messy picture of leadership.

Greg and I stopped at a local Chinese restaurant, famished and physically exhausted but still emotionally keyed up from catching more fish than we'd ever seen in our lives. Few people were in the restaurant, so we had a small room on the side all to ourselves. Greg is a great guy with a wonderful sense of humor, and we were laughing and talking about some of the fishing miscues we'd already made. That's when I spotted the small boy, who couldn't have been over four years old, running into our room, holding a chocolate ice-cream cone.

Actually, he wasn't exactly holding it. The little boy looked like a Hershey bar had exploded all over him. Chocolate was smeared across his face, and coated his hand and clothes as well. The boy apparently saw what looked to him like a large napkin—my pant leg! Without saying a word, he ran over to our table and proceeded to wipe his mouth and little face on my pants.

I jumped up, shocked at what had happened, and said, "Hey, kid . . . what do you think you're doing?" Still without speaking, he rushed toward me again to wipe his face on my pant leg.

I held out my hand and kept him away, and he took a step back. Just then his mother and father rounded the corner. "Look what your kid did!" I said, pointing to my newly smeared pants. That's when the little angel drew back and threw what was left of his ice-cream cone at me and hit me right in the chest!

While I was considering pressing charges against this incorrigible four year old, Greg was nearly falling down with laughter! Meanwhile, the little boy triumphantly walked back to his parents and stood between them, never saying a word.

"What are you going to do about this!" I asked the parents, still in disbelief at what had happened. There was a long pause, the parents looked at each other, and finally the mother said to her precious darling, "Come on, sweetheart, we'll have to get you another ice-cream cone." And they turned and walked out of the room.

To this day, I marvel at what happened that night. With the kind of leadership this mom and dad offered, I'm sure that by now that boy is already leading his own Colombian drug cartel—or maybe he's running for Congress. As bad as having chocolate all over my pants was having to put up with Greg telling and retelling the story to our whole group (and anyone else who would listen). But that traumatic experience did teach me an important lesson: Always realize who it is who *really* loses in a home where leadership from the parents is fragmented or nonexistent—it's little four year olds who grow up without godly models. When a husband and wife are unwilling to have clear leadership roles between them, it will have lasting consequences for their relationship and for their children.

Leadership between a husband and a wife will either create confusion and conflict (when roles are unclear or abandoned) or a welcome stability in their marriage and a lasting, positive legacy to and through their children.

The sixth way to lasting love is adopting and accepting a leadership style that draws the couple together so they can face the realities and challenges that life brings. The husband leads and the wife follows, yet she expresses her individuality and influences her husband's decisions. It's like two figure skaters.

My family and I enjoy watching the Olympic ice skating every four years, especially the pairs competition. Anytime ice skating is broadcast on television, my wife and daughters are glued to the set, and I confess even I enjoy watching the Olympic finals, whether it's the solo figure skaters, like Brian Boitano or Nancy Kerrigan, or the graceful yet sophisticated moves of pairs skaters.

Part of the beauty and attraction of pair skating is how effortlessly these couples move and flow together. One taking the lead, two skating together. That image reflects a picture of leadership that Solomon's bride gives us. In Song of Songs 1:4, the future bride gives a beautiful and insightful look at leadership in their home in the form of a pointed request: "Draw me after you and let us run together."

Sometimes the most is said in the fewest words. That's true in the above nine-word description of biblical roles and responsibilities in a marriage. She begins by asking him to move out front to "draw me after you." But before you slam down the book and write off what she says as just another power play for intolerant, male dominance emanating from a pre-industrial, hierarchical society—remember this is *God's* Word. Look closely at exactly what she's asking him to "take the lead" in doing, and you will see this is not a case of dominance but of proper, godly leadership.

"DRAW ME AFTER YOU"

If anyone should have been hesitant to ask a man to take the lead, it would have been Solomon's bride. She had endured years of mistreatment in her family business, working under those "angry brothers." Surely she had grounds for including a prenuptial clause that said, "Nobody, *but nobody*, is going to control me!" Yet here she asks not to be pathologically controlled or physically dominated, but to be lovingly drawn by him. Hers is a request that honors both men and women.[1]

> *God draws His people with "bonds of love." Put another way, He ... takes the lead in loving them.*

The Hebrew word for *draw* is chock-full of meaning. It can describe the unique, special, love relationship God has with His people. "I led them [literally, 'I drew them'] with cords of a man, with bonds of love," God tells Hosea, "and I became to them as one who lifts the yoke from their jaws; and I bent down and fed them" (Hosea 11:4). In Song of Songs 1:4, as in the description in Hosea, Solomon's bride is asking him to take the lead in doing something God Himself does, something that in no way could be construed as ruthless control. God draws His people with "bonds of love." Put another way, He gets in front of them and takes the lead in loving them.

Draw also is used in Hosea 11 to picture God as an ever-serving guide who faithfully led the Israelites through the desert to a place of green grass and fresh water as He promised. Moses captures God's own words in describing this time: "I have led you forty years in the wilderness; your clothes have not worn out on you, and your sandal has not worn out on your foot" (Deuteronomy 29:5). That adds the traits of a willing servant to that of taking the lead in love.

A third usage of the word *draw* is found in Jeremiah 31:3. God speaks to His people and says, "I have loved you with an everlasting love; therefore *I have drawn you* with lovingkindness" (emphasis added). In other words, God's love is filled with constant expressions of His mercy, care, and compassion. Put all three uses of "draw me" together and look what she's asking him to do. She desires that her husband be like her heavenly Father by:

- *Taking the lead in loving her*
- *Taking the lead in guiding them as husband and wife toward God's best*
- *Taking the lead in serving her*
- *Taking the lead in sensitivity, compassion, and care*

Men, if you were to show these particular male leadership traits to your wife, I doubt that you'd meet with a great deal of resistance from her. Women, if your husbands were committed to showing you this type of sacrificial love, would you be more or less likely to trust and respect their leadership in other areas of your life?

". . . AND LET US RUN TOGETHER"

A man who responds to God's leadership in his life and then reflects godly leadership traits in his home adds to the strength of the family and gives his wife confidence, strength, and freedom to be herself. And remember, it's not *him demanding* to lead. It's *her asking*, and she's not through with her request. Yes, she asks him to draw them out onto the ice, but once the lights go on and the music begins . . . it's pairs skating all the way.

My wife, Cindy, is a friend, a confidante, an encourager, a romantic, and a great mother. She's also a strong person. She persevered to become the first person in her family to gain a college degree and then a postgraduate (master's) degree. She was an outstanding teacher (and remains an outstanding Sunday school teacher). She has a strong sense of right and wrong, so that she stood up before hundreds at our school board meeting when they sought to push through a horrible sex education curriculum. She's strong enough that when I have to go on a trip, I have never once in seventeen years worried, "What if something happened to one of the kids, the car, or the house?" And she's strong enough to know that God's Word is right. In our home, I set the pace, but the two of us skate together.

Though one skater leads during the pair competition, both are equal in aptitude and intelligence. Similarly in marriage, there is no inferiority of person, intelligence, or spiritual insight between the husband and wife. When the couple is skating in unison, everyone can see it, from the parents to the children, and even the family dog. But when they skate independently of each other, the couple is out of sync, and an eventual collision can result.

In her beautiful description of their teamwork, the bride of Solomon draws us a picture of the young lovers running hand in hand, keeping the same pace and maintaining the same rhythm. It's a portrait of two people in harmony, working together to accomplish what God wants for them and their family. Sadly, too many times, couples are running into or away from each other. Loving couples, though, strike a godly balance in leadership, and the result is another element of intimacy, pure and true.

WHY MEN DO NOT LEAD

There are great benefits to following her words. She advocates a biblical style of leadership in the home that can clarify husband-and-wife roles and make sure that family responsibilities are not ignored. But if such a leadership style is so mutually beneficial, we need to answer a few questions. Questions like, "What's holding men back from taking the lead?" and, "What factors keep a woman from being drawn or running together with her husband?" Let's begin by answering the first question.

Without question, one of the most common complaints I hear from Christian wives is that men aren't taking the lead. Although there are certainly exceptions, it's often not the wife who is blocking the husband from loving, serving, and nurturing her and the family—it's him! What holds a man back from stepping out front . . . even when she's asking? Let's look at a few reasons behind an issue we could study at length (and some men need to).[2]

1. Stored-Up Anger

Most men live with some (or a large) degree of unresolved anger in their lives. You can see that in the ways it comes out—like when they're driving! I once heard of a father who drove his kids to school one day, and then the next day his wife drove them. As the mother was getting the little boy out of the car, he looked up at her and said, "Mommy . . . where are all the idiots today?"

"*What*, honey?" she said, in shock.

"The idiots, Mom. Where are they?"

"Honey, what in the world are you talking about?"

"Well, yesterday Daddy drove us to school, and we saw seven idiots!"

If you think *that's* funny, the anger men hold inside can often have more comic (and tragic) results. In his book, *Angry Men, Passive Men*, Marvin Allen tells that in one calendar year alone (1993), fourteen men across the country were crushed to death by soft drink machines![3] It's easy to imagine what happened. They were so infuriated when the vending machine didn't give them their cola, they decided to take matters into their own hands and attack the machine. In the process of yanking on the machine to get their drink, it fell on them and crushed them to death.

Men with stored-up anger risk danger, and not just by avenging soda machines. Sinful anger, held inside, can leap out and destroy a man's ability to lead. Sinful anger is an explosion of emotions waiting to happen. When we're angry at our spouse or our kids, the first thing on our minds is not being loving or sensitive. It's getting some barrier out of our way, forcing someone to buckle in on a decision we don't want to discuss, or defending our selfish pride when we're convicted.

*Sinful anger, held inside, can leap out
and destroy a man's ability to lead.*

There's nothing wrong with getting angry over the things God gets angry about. (If that weren't true, then Christ would not be without sin for we're told He "became angry"; nor could we explain the many times God the Father's "anger burned" toward unrighteousness.) It was righteous anger that won the terrible battle in the trenches in France at Belle Woods in World War I. Righteous anger over Pearl Harbor fueled victories at Palermo, Normandy, and Iwo Jima in World War II. Righteous indignation shut down Saddam Hussein and locked up an older-era gangster named Al Capone.

Capone's Mafia rule of Chicago during Prohibition was complete and unquestioned by even law authorities. Then one Christian layman named Frank Lehey, angry over the lawlessness in the streets and independent of any local law enforcement or government agency, set up the Chicago Crime Commission. His work, at great threat to his own and his family's life, brought great honor to Christ and airtight indictments that finally put Capone away for life.

There is a time when we have to be strong, and God has given men that extra dose of adrenaline to draw on when we must be warriors. But too many families are victims of "friendly fire," when a man takes out unrighteous anger at home.

When it comes to men and anger, there's good news and bad news. The bad news is many men, myself included, have struggled with it. At a men's retreat I taught several years ago, the men were given the choice of attending any one of five afternoon workshops. Topics ranged from gaining financial freedom to increasing quiet time clout, to dealing with anger. Out of the 300 men at the retreat, guess how many went to the seminar on controlling anger? If you guessed 275, you're right. (And the other 25 guys were ticked off because the room was too small for all of them to fit in.)

Men can and do struggle with anger. But the good news is that there is more help and more hope than ever to keep anger within biblical boundaries. Psalm 37:7–8 says, "Rest in the Lord and wait patiently for Him. . . . Cease from anger and forsake wrath; do not fret, it leads only to evildoing."

If you're a man whose anger is blocking you from taking the lead God's way (with love, service, and sensitivity), then get help. Talk to your pastor. Meet with an outstanding Christian counselor in your area. Join a weekly men's group like CrossTrainers. Go to a Promise Keepers conference. Or do what I do: anytime you raise your voice at your kids in anger, apologize immediately and instantly pay them one dollar. I've done this for a number of years, and to my shame and discredit, the first week I instituted that policy my girls were on their way to Harvard! I had to learn to deal with anger or go broke—so I've worked very hard at it. I hardly ever lose even a single dollar now, but I continue to work on that area by reading outstanding books such as Gary Oliver's *Real Men Have Feelings Too* and Oliver and Norm Wright's book, *When Anger Hits Home.*

Unchecked anger can build up and blow—and destroy your base for godly leadership in the home. So too can never having had a model at home to pattern after.

2. The Lack of Models and Mentors

I had all kinds of models of leadership growing up: John Wayne, Mickey Mantle, Paul Hourning. The problem was, they were on television showing one side of their character, not at home where I could watch them twenty-four hours a day. What I needed was a godly mentor. Someone I could see up close and personal, model myself after, and call and ask questions if I were stuck in a slump.

For many men, thank the Lord, that mentor has been their father. I meet many such men at the Promise Keepers conferences I speak at where often two and even *three* generations are represented! Unfortunately, there are also way too many men like me.

*It hurts if we don't have a father. But it helps
to have a slightly older man in our life
who walks the walk, and can teach us how.*

At the 1995 Indianapolis Promise Keepers conference I made a pointed request to all 62,000 men. "If you're like me," I said, "and you've grown up in a home without a father for the majority of your growing-up years, I'd like to ask you to stand up right now." I was shocked by the response. Perhaps 25,000 men—more than one-third of the men in the stadium—stood to their feet. I had the rest of the men then stand and put their hands on the shoulders of these father-less men as we prayed for them. Then we went on and talked about how to be a father who gives the "blessing" to his children.

It hurts if we don't have a father. But it helps to have a slightly older man in our life who walks the walk, and can teach us how. I thank God that at various times in my life, He's given me several such men to stand in for my father. Men like my spiritual father, Doug Barram, and Howard Hendricks, whose outstanding example is the reason I went into family ministry.

If you need to know what a "mentor" looks like, I recommend the excellent book by Howard Hendricks and his son Bill, *As Iron Sharpens Iron*. They will challenge you men to ask God to bring an older man into your life who is *still* walking the walk. To spend as much time as you can with him, ask him a thousand questions. Call him when you need advice, and ask him to pray earnestly for you. You'll appreciate it, and your wife will rave about it.

3. Fear of Failure

Deep down inside, it isn't snakes, prostate cancer, and losing our hair that most men fear—it is failure. For most of us, failure isn't just a missed opportunity. It's not knowing how to succeed, be it in our business or personal life.

Failure paralyzes many of us, so much that we can be too

afraid to try something new (like taking the spiritual lead of our home). In other words, thinking *What if I fail?* keeps us from believing *I know I'll succeed.* For men who don't feel they have a clue as to how to successfully lead their families, the fear of trying and failing can leave them moored on a sandbar of procrastination and self-doubt.

Warren Bennis, in his book *On Becoming a Leader*, notes that not only is leadership more an expression of our character than our position, a willingness to lead also reflects our ability to view failure as an opportunity.[4] Of the hundreds of successful leaders that Bennis interviewed over the years, one of the common themes that emerged was their ability to see failure not as a commentary on their value, but as an excuse to learn, grow, and adapt. "Don't fear failure," as one leader put it, "fear *not trying.*"

That's solid advice. Satan wants nothing more than to snag all of us in the quicksand of fear-based procrastination. He wants us to believe that because of our experience, upbringing, or surroundings, we can't step out in faith. But Satan's a liar (John 8:44). Under the direction and guidance of God's Holy Spirit and with the help and support of caring Christians, failure doesn't have to be a billboard on the road of your future. You *can* answer the call to godly leadership in your home—and know that God will equip you every step of the way for success.

4. Waiting for the Call to Action

Another limitation that many men face is waiting for the bugle to sound "charge" before they are willing to get up and move. Ever since the early sixties, all the cultural confusion we've experienced has sounded like a hundred different bugle calls. Some special interest groups have played at full volume, "There's something innately wrong with being a man." Others have sounded the notes, "You have no right to lead." Still others trumpeted, "Men are worthless! Look at all the damage you've done!" With all the blaring noise, any positive, redeeming male traits or accomplishments have been discounted or dismissed. Most men have felt the safest place to be is "missing in action" instead of in the thick of the fight.

> *Men today are ripe for a clarion call.*
> *They're ready to be challenged.*

That's one of the reasons I think the Promise Keepers movement has been highly successful. Men today are ripe for a clarion call. They're ready to be challenged. They've waited for years for someone to clearly say, "Get up and get moving! You've been under fire (much of it justified by your sinful anger), but the way off the beach and to victory is to stand up, shoulder your responsibilities before Christ, and fight for what's right!"

The trumpet is sounding *now*, calling husbands to lead their wives and fathers to lead their families. It's time to answer the call. You've got your marching orders—to lead in love, service, and sensitivity. Now let's get at it!

WHAT KEEPS WOMEN FROM ASKING FOR OR "RUNNING ALONGSIDE" LEADERSHIP?

We've looked at four things that keep men from taking the lead, yet there's another side to this issue as well. Many women across our country have rallied their family to live for Christ long before men were rallying in stadiums. However, it would be wrong to assume that there aren't things that can hold women back from looking to their husbands for leadership or "running together" with them in daily life. Let's look at three challenges women face in following this sixth way of love and responding to effective leadership. (And for you men readers, keep reading to gain a window into her world as well.)

1. Dominating Men

Sydney Pollack, famous movie director and screenwriter, made an interesting observation about being a director: "Up to a point," he said, "I think you can lead out of fear and intimidation, as awful as that sounds. You can make people follow you by scaring them. . . . But the problem is you're creating obedience with *a residue of resentment*" (emphasis mine).[5]

If that's true on the movie set, it's doubly true in a home. Some women have grown up with a "residue of resentment" for any type of male leadership because of the way their father, stepfather, or other male figure has dominated them in the past. Men are to lead, not to dominate. That resentment can even flare right after a honeymoon!

Maria met her husband, Ruben, when both were missionaries serving with Campus Crusade for Christ. They had become best friends and now lovers. But Maria blew up two days after their honeymoon. Why? Maria came from a tyrannical non-Christian home, with a father who worked with her two older brothers as a "sheetrocker." After taping and floating Sheetrock® (or drywall) all day, they would burst open the door around four o'clock in the afternoon, strip, and throw their clothes everywhere while they showered and cleaned up. Then they demanded dinner on the table at 5 o'clock sharp. From there, it was off to "pound down some 'brewskies'" at the local tavern before stumbling in and waking everyone up late at night.

That pattern went on day after day—and day after day guess who was expected to clean up and cook for the men of that family? That's right, Maria and her mother. There's nothing wrong with cooking and cleaning, but in their home, it was neither appreciated nor valued . . . and neither were they. Now let's fast-forward the tape. Maria is now an outstanding Christian, involved in ministry, and married to a wonderful Christian man. Yet they had been home from their honeymoon only two days when the "residue of resentment" she carried acted like leftover gasoline fumes and ignited.

"Pick those up!" she almost screamed at Ruben. He was so startled by her angry words, he nearly jumped off the sofa where he'd been sitting. "You pick up those socks!" she said, her lip quivering.

"Honey, what's wrong?" Ruben said, still confused. Sure, he'd just taken his shoes and socks off, but he'd just sat down on the sofa to watch a television program. Never before in their two-year friendship or six-month engagement had he seen that flash of anger. But it was there, waiting for the right trigger mechanism. When she saw her young husband drop his socks on the floor, it reminded her of years of having to pick up clothes for men who didn't appreciate her. The unresolved resentment flamed anew.

Socks tossed on the carpet may seem like a trivial thing, but it led to one of the best discussions and prayer times Maria and Ruben had ever experienced. That's because Maria was suddenly confronted with a level of inner resentment that lay in her life.

Your present perspective on a hurtful past can make all the difference in how powerfully it grips you.

What's a woman to do to get rid of such resentment? If you believe you have such resentment, first admit it's there and confront the fact that it can make you instantly defensive toward even minor imperfections or attempts by your husband to lead. Second, try to directly confront past wrongs if there is the opportunity or time. We've already talked about the need to "go back home" in the chapters on "leaving," so be sure to review that material if necessary. And third, realize that your present perspective on a hurtful past can make all the difference in how powerfully it grips you.[6]

All the things that happened to Maria in her past certainly weren't good. But as she and Ruben dug out and faced the buried resentment that was there, they found that, indeed, God had brought "great good" to their marriage. What about you?

Are there hidden resentments you're carrying as a wife? They can certainly keep you from "running together" and at arm's length from a loving husband's leadership.

2. Great Expectations

Think about it. Most Disney movies have been structured around a wonderfully successful premise: Love conquers all.

In spite of incredible obstacles and temptations, a woman's love finally wins out. What's more, she is proven right in nearly losing it all to gain him. He *is* worth fighting for. He is a beauty, not a beast. From *Snow White* and *Sleeping Beauty* to *Beauty and the Beast* and *Pocahontas*, true love happens, and it does not require effort to maintain. While this makes for wonderfully entertaining theater (and draws on deeply felt needs and emotions), such attitudes can bring incredibly damaging expectations to a marriage.

Remember our first picture of love, in which Solomon's bride praises the soundness of his character, saying, "Your name is like purified oil"? How many women have clearly seen and yet still married a "beast," knowing "There's just got to be a 'beauty' in there somewhere!" Not only in mate selection, but in expecting a mate to be as romantic as Prince Charming or as witty or wise as a cartoon character, a woman can set herself up for disappointment. Let's face it. Real men come complete with real imperfections. Even if we've worked hard on our character like Solomon did, and we have a good "name," we're *not* going to be perfect. And we're not just talking about snoring here. Minor lapses in sensitivity, serving, or loving our spouse can happen as well.

Men are fallible humans! And as such, a great gift you wives can give your husband is unconditional love and tolerance for his emotional weaknesses. Here's what I mean: If your husband is faithful to you to a fault, completes 90 percent of the assigned chores, takes the children to church and the park, works hard at his job—but he takes over the television set for Monday night football and refuses to talk during the fourth quarter—cut him some emotional slack! Give him four quarters of high-fiving time once a week all his own. As heretical as it may sound, even a weekend of fishing with the "guys" (or better yet, going to a Promise Keepers conference) *without your resentment* can bring him back more energized and ready to love and serve you.

No, I am not saying to overlook immorality or become pathologically "co-dependent" by urging him to go fishing for the weekend when he hasn't spent a minute of time with you and the kids. If you're facing marital problems up to your neck, all his spare time and money should be spent with you in counseling, not on the lake. But if a man is showing you real love with real consistency—the kind of love James would say makes him a "doer of the word, and not merely [a] hearer" (1:22)—then reward his maleness with appreciation and respect as Solomon's bride did.

3. Resentment and Anger

If you listen to the media, women are at war with men. Christina Hoff Sommers, herself a self-proclaimed feminist, has written an outstanding book called *Who Stole Feminism?* and subtitled *How Women Have Betrayed Women*. Sommers argues that the call for a continued hatred of men is divorced from the lives of the majority of women. She is reacting to "gender feminists," represented in such books as *The War Against Women*, which "lays out women's state in this world—and it is a state of siege."[7] Speaking of gender feminists, Sommers writes: "They see themselves as the second wave of the feminist movement, as the moral vanguard fighting a war to save women."[8]

She quotes feminist Marilyn French's portrayal of "ordinary men" engaging in ongoing female oppression:

> As long as some men use physical force to subjugate females, *all* men need not. The knowledge that some men do suffices to threaten all women. . . . [A man can] beat or kill the woman he claims to love; he can rape women, whether mate, acquaintance, or stranger; he can rape or sexually molest his daughters, nieces, stepchildren, or the children of a woman he claims to love. *The vast majority of men in the world do one or more of the above.* (French's emphasis)[9]

Can you get a glimpse of the culture of anger and continued resentment that the radical feminist movement is advocating through books and women's study programs? Gender feminists are adored and promoted in the mainstream media, and their target is men, *all* men. For men are evil, and if a woman is unlucky enough to marry one, she is pulling down doom upon herself. Some men, argue feminists, abuse women physically, verbally, and emotionally—and all men can abuse—so women must avoid them in long-term relationships.

I know across the country there are thousands of men who have abused their wives or children. Abuse is intolerable and indefensible. Such men should be prosecuted to the full extent of the law (and then turned over to the general prison population where even there they're considered the lowest of the low). But are you ready to base your life on the statement, "Because some do . . . all women are threatened"? Every week *millions* of men across this country go to church, work hard, and go to their graves without ever once having acted that way.

Sommers and other women authors, such as Daphne Patai and Noretta Koertge in *Professing Feminism*, show how women are deserting the radical gender feminist message in droves. And a balanced, biblical perspective on a woman's proper, exalted relationship among men exists in such books as *Women of Honor*, by Jean Hendricks, or *Mom! You're Incredible!* by Lindy Weber.

We've seen the encouragement Solomon's bride has given him to lead in a loving way so that the two of them may "run together." May her words—and this way of love—be the model you strive for with each other and present before your children. If it is, I can guarantee that if your four year old throws his ice-cream cone at a stranger—he will do it only once!

CHAPTER 13

Principle #7

BUILDING YOUR LIFE
ACCORDING TO CODE

Growing up in a single-parent home, I never had a father to instruct me in using tools or working in cars, so I entered our marriage "mechanically challenged." In contrast, Cindy's father and brothers were all Mr. Goodwrenches. They could overhaul complete engines, do major body work, and repair Apollo moon vehicles if called on. That's why Cindy was so insistent that I change the oil in our car.

"Honey," I argued, "If I change the oil myself, it'll take jobs away from the Quick Lube people. That's going to hurt our local economy, cause some poor guy to lose his job, and maybe even put his kids out on the street! You don't want *that* on your conscience, do you?" My precious wife wasn't buying that excuse, especially when a television commercial came on for Valvoline oil where they actually had a *monkey* do an oil change!

"See there!" Cindy pointed, nearly coming out of her chair. "If a monkey can change the oil, I know you can do it!" Motivated by her confidence in my intelligence and natural aptitudes, I thought to myself, *I can do it! I can change the oil! No monkey's going to make a monkey out of me!*

That Saturday afternoon, I went next door where my very

patient neighbor lived and borrowed several wrenches, hammers, crowbars, and other miscellaneous tools. ("This is all stuff you need when you're changing the oil *yourself*," I assured him.) Did I ask my neighbor for instructions? Did I check out a car repair book? Absolutely not. That would have been a sign of weakness! Instead, proving once again that "man is more advanced than the ape," I crawled under the car, and right in front of my eyes was a very large bolt. *That's it!* I thought to myself, *I found it!*

I took my wrench, unscrewed the bolt, and out poured red oil. I quickly got a pan under the gushing fluid, and I can remember thinking to myself, *Boy, it's a good thing I'm changing the oil, because when oil gets really old, it must turn red!* After the last drop was drained, I screwed back in the bolt, wiped off my hands, and proceeded to pour eight quarts of oil into the engine.

Cindy was shocked when I walked back into the house in less than an hour all washed up, with the tools returned, and the oil changed. As you can imagine, she was especially proud of me that night for attempting a mechanical task, and I was seriously thinking about renewing my subscription to *Car and Driver* or maybe even *Mechanics Illustrated*. That is, until Sunday morning, when Cindy and I were driving down the Central Expressway in Dallas after a late departure for church. It was about a twenty-minute drive, but about five miles down the road, we began to smell something funny. A few more miles down the road the car began to shake violently.

If you haven't guessed by now, when I changed that red "oil," I'd made a slight mistake. Instead of oil, I had actually drained out every drop of our *transmission* fluid! That meant, with the oil I'd added, I had roughly sixteen quarts of oil in our car and a major problem on my hands. Like a frozen transmission and engine damage! Right in the middle of Central Expressway on our way to church!!! We were thankful I had picked Sunday morning, instead of Friday rush hour, to destroy our car; yet I think it would be fair to say that Cindy never insisted that I change the oil myself again.

Later, after our car had been towed to a repair shop, I saw my mistake. There, underneath the car, were *two* bolts and two pans, almost the same size, and very close to each other. All I'd done was mixed up one little bolt! In hindsight, I have to admit that if only I had broken down and looked at instructions in the owner's manual, I would have saved us hundreds of dollars and hours of inconvenience and hassle.

The principle is the same in flying an aircraft. The next time you're on an airplane, as you enter, peek into the pilot's cabin and watch the pilot and copilot going through their flight list . . . step by step. The two have a lengthy preflight checklist, and they won't ignore one item. Everything must check out according to the book. When you see a videotape of the next launch of the space shuttle, ask yourself if Mission Control just "winged it" in the countdown procedure to blast-off—or went through an exhaustive man and computer checklist.

In every case, a successful oil change, a plane trip, or a shuttle launch can be traced to doing things "by the book." The same thing is true in construction of a house. An architect draws a set of plans that conform to rules of structural integrity and local zoning regulations. Then a wise builder will build "according to code." That's true whether he or she is building a house—or a marriage.

BUILDING WITH THE RIGHT MATERIALS

Our seventh principle of a lasting love appears in Song of Songs 1:16–17. The bride-to-be returns a compliment that Solomon has just given her. In verse 15, he said, "How beautiful you are, my darling, how beautiful you are! Your eyes are like doves."

We looked at this verse earlier and saw that when Solomon described his bride's eyes this way, he was doing much more than simply affirming her gentle and quiet spirit. He was also referring to her godliness and how her eyes reflected God's Spirit.

Not to be outdone, she gives him a like compliment:

161

"How handsome you are, my beloved, and so pleasant! Indeed, our couch is luxuriant! The beams of our houses are cedars, our rafters, cypresses." (1:16–17)

There's no doubt she's affirming his physical appearance —to her he is a hunk! But she says much more with her unusual choice of words and pictures. He has just praised her for her beauty *and* her spirituality. She acknowledges how handsome he is *and* also how committed he is to "build" their relationship with godly materials. Our seventh principle is to build godly lives by knowing and following God's guidebook for living, the Bible. While in chapter 4 we noted that the foundation for building character is knowing God through His Son Jesus, now the materials for building godliness are those things that draw us close to God—studying His Word, prayer, and acts of service.

In mentioning cedars and cypresses, Solomon's bride uses rich, royal imagery. Such woods were the finest of their day, used almost exclusively in the construction of God's tabernacle and throughout the temple in Jerusalem. She also speaks of these materials being the load-bearing "beams and rafters" that will keep a roof over their heads and their house together. One can see a similar "picture" of another building analogy that the apostle Paul used several centuries later.

According to the grace of God which was given to me, like a wise master builder I laid a foundation, and another is building on it. But each man must be careful how he builds on it. For no man can lay a foundation other than the one which is laid, which is Jesus Christ. Now if any man builds on the foundation with gold, silver, precious stones, wood, hay, straw, each man's work will become evident; for the day will show it because it is to be revealed with fire, and the fire itself will test the quality of each man's work. (1 Corinthians 3:10–13)

How do homebuilders construct beautiful homes? It takes planning, perseverance, and choosing the best materials to build a house that will last a lifetime. Similarly, you choose quality materials—ones that meet the code for godly living to build a life—and a marriage—that will last. It takes the right set of plans—God's Holy Bible—and the right building materials—like prayer and worship—to build a home to "God's code" of distinctive holiness. And it takes something else as well: hard work, consistency, and obedience to follow the plan.

THE MYTH OF THE SPIRITUAL LOTTERY

Across our country, "lottery fever" is running a 104-degree temperature. More state legislators accept the lottery as a way to help state budgets with needed funds; more gamblers see it as harmless fun, though it eats up their funds. One could say "it's just a dollar," but it's also a clear reflection of how much people want achievement without effort. What a lottery promises is to make someone an "instant" millionaire (or in the larger lotteries, a millionaire many times over). The promise is always that you can put down a dollar today and wake up with a fortune tomorrow.

> *We need to be reminded to slow down, to build with care, to choose building materials that can last a lifetime.*

I'm convinced that when it comes to their spiritual lives, way too many Christians are doing exactly the same thing. They're investing one dollar of effort and time in seeking God and looking to His Word, and then expecting to wake up one day rich in spiritual maturity and "Christ-centeredness." Many couples say they want a better spiritual life but don't take steps to get there.

It takes real effort to grow spiritually. In our "instant everything" society with microwaves, automatic teller machines, and instant oatmeal, we're used to getting what we want and getting it *now*. If we don't, we quickly become frustrated. We need to be reminded to slow down, to build with care, to choose building materials that can last a lifetime.

HOW TO BUILD

Let's look at how to do that when it comes to building up our spiritual lives. Get ready for real work, not the lottery. Such work, though, is worth it. Years later you will gaze upon a beautiful, God-blessed spiritual structure that protects your spouse and children.

1. Invest Your Time

In the 1990s, we are tyrannized by time constraints. The average work week increased from 40.6 hours in 1973 to 46.6 hours in 1987, and it continues to edge upward.[1] We're working longer and harder than ever. I realize that just mentioning one more thing that cuts into your time can make you feel like closing this chapter (or throwing the book across the room). But don't!

> *God is not someone you make time for in your schedule. God is our schedule.*

The first step to a refreshing and dynamic spiritual life together is to realize that God is not someone you make time for in your schedule. God *is* your schedule. He's the most important part of your day. Without Him, you couldn't breathe, much less sell cars, build houses, or teach school. He is sovereignly in control of everything in your life and as such deserves first place in everything.

So, as a couple, you have a fundamental decision to make. Are you willing to spend time with Him on a regular basis? Are you willing to give Him priority in your schedule, both together and separately? There are so many benefits if you do, for both you and your children.

Recently, I've been on a number of "call in" radio programs across the country, talking about the subject of integrity and people who depict that quality. When I asked the listeners in three different cities to call in with the name and stories of someone in their life who most exemplified a person of godly character, I received three identical calls. This wasn't the same person calling from three different cities, but three different people saying the very same thing: "My father is my example of character."

When I asked them to be a little more specific, their answers were identical. "When I would get up in the morning as a child," they'd say, "I'd walk out and see my dad sitting there, reading his Bible. I never realized what he was doing until years later, but he was starting his day out with God's Word."

What a legacy it leaves your children if you'll carve out time for God's Word. And what a great suggestion to start your day out by focusing on Him.

2. Get a Spiritual Start to Your Day

It's extremely important to get off to a good start. A clear picture of that came in the wonderful movie *Chariots of Fire*, the true story of Olympic athlete Eric Liddell. In the movie, Sam Mussabini is a noted track coach who goes up to Scotland to "scout" the "Flying Scotsman," an incredible athlete and an equally outstanding Christian.

In the race the coach watched, Liddell was accidentally tripped in the opening turn. But the determined athlete got off the ground to catch up and win the race. Exhausted by the monumental effort, Liddell fell to the ground, and Mussabini hurried over and helped pick him up. "It was not the prettiest quarter I've ever seen," he told the Scotsman. "But it was the bravest."

Making up ground in a race is possible—especially if you're an Olympic-class athlete. But it's doubly hard to do in the "race toward the prize of the high calling in Jesus Christ" that we're called to run. When we fail to begin our day with prayer and God's Word, it's like we're starting the daily race from behind. Then when the pressures of the day trip us up, we're not in any kind of shape to get up and finish well for our Savior.

God is a God of grace, and one of the ways He reflects that is in giving us liberty and freedom to make choices in many areas of life. That includes when or if we decide to set aside a specific time to spend with Him. I'm not saying you have to have a quiet time in the morning (though from personal experience and years of observing close-knit Christian couples, I know there's often a common denominator of beginning their day with God's Word). The important thing is to spend time with Him on a regular basis. But what does "getting into His Word" really mean?

3. Make His Word Central

Right after I became a Christian in high school, I was told by the man who led me to Christ to go to a Christian bookstore and get a Bible. I vividly remember walking into a Christian bookstore for the very first time—and walking away confused and upset. My only experience at looking at and buying books had been at a secular bookstore, where you had to be very discerning of what you picked up. But you also need to be discerning in choosing spiritual books. After entering the Christian bookstore, I soon became very nervous about making a mistake and picking the wrong Bible!

When we read the Bible, we are, in effect, hearing God speak to us. In it, He shares His heart, His desires, His pain, and His wisdom.

I finally picked up a *New American Standard Bible* with a blue cover and took it over to the man at the register. I asked him if it was a "good" Bible.

"Yes it is, son," he said. "But I can't sell it to you."

"Uhhhh . . . come again?" I said. "You can't sell it to me?"

"No, I can't. You see, this Bible has a blue cover on it, and everyone knows that the only *good* Bible is one that's *read*."

I'm sure if I'd been a Christian for a few years, I'd have

instantly picked up his "Christian humor." But I didn't. I stood there confused, trying to figure out if "good" Bibles really did come only with red covers. I'd seen a few Bibles on the shelves with red covers, but I didn't like them. I liked the blue one. But now I was so embarrassed and confused that I turned around and walked out of the store!

Today, I can laugh about what happened and about his play on words. And actually he was right! The best Bible *is* one that's read (like the blue one with my name on it that is sitting here on my desk). When we read the Bible, we are, in effect, hearing God speak to us. In it, He shares His heart, His desires, His pain, and His wisdom. It took Him well over a thousand years and dozens of willing servants inspired by His Holy Spirit to capture His message of salvation and sanctification.

Here are three ideas about how to make your time in God's Word count. *First, make sure you understand the difference between a translation and a paraphrase.* Translations are made directly from the best available Hebrew and Greek manuscripts and attempt to convey the meaning of the text as accurately as possible. (Hebrew is the original language of the Old Testament, and Greek is the language of the New Testament.) Examples of translations are the *New American Standard Bible* (NASB), the *New King James Version* (NKJV), and the *New International Version* (NIV). A translation should be your "study" Bible and the first place you go to read a passage.

Then there are also any number of good interpretive *paraphrases* that have come out, from *The Living Bible*, by Ken Taylor to J. B. Phillip's translation and a new interpretive version called simply *The Message* (by Eugene Peterson). These are wonderfully readable ways of looking at the Scriptures, but realize they are "interpretations." They may offer you valuable help in making sense of a difficult passage by offering that person's insights (much like a Bible commentary would), but they are not word by word accurate. As dynamic paraphrases of the actual wording, they represent a great way to supplement your Bible reading. However, a readable paraphrase is not infallible, so be sure in your study time to include an accurate translation of the Bible (which is available in *many* different colors).

Second, buy a concordance. This is an invaluable tool that lists all the uses of virtually every word in the Old and New Testaments. For instance, a concordance can help you locate every place where the word *beloved* is used in the Song of Songs for your own study of the meaning and uses of the word. Or, if you wanted to learn more about the Bible's perspective on a particular subject like heaven, hell, riches, marriage, or wisdom, you could turn to any of those words, and have a field day looking up scores of verses.

One of the first Christian books I ever read was Hal Lindsey's *The Late Great Planet Earth*. Being too young in the faith to know you *didn't* have to do it, I stopped and looked up every verse in my brand-new Bible and concordance (and there were *hundreds* of verses) that accompanied a statement in the book. I learned more about God's Word looking up verses in my concordance than I did from the book itself! If you run across a word or phrase you don't understand or want to learn more about, use a concordance to discover more. (Be sure, though, to purchase a concordance that corresponds to your translation of the Bible. For instance, if you use a *New American Standard Bible*, buy an NASB concordance.)

Third, spend time alone and together in the Scriptures. Help each other stay accountable. It's also important to guard each other's time against interruptions. For instance, if you've decided that immediately after the children go to bed is the best time to read and pray, ask your spouse to take phone calls, let out the dog, or handle anything else that comes up during that period of time.

"For Christ, prayer wasn't preparation for battle, prayer was the battle."

When you spend time together, include prayer, sharing of concerns, worship, and talking about what you've been learning on your own in God's Word. I highly recommend a brief journal of your *individual* time so you'll have a ready reminder when you share together. You can also use that journal to record what the *two of you* share. Looking back over your thoughts, prayers, and impressions is a great way to see how God has worked in your life.

Believe me, I know that it can be hard to carve out an unhurried time to pray. When he was a professor at Dallas Seminary, Haddon Robinson once told us, "For Christ, prayer wasn't preparation for the battle, prayer *was* the battle." Many of us can attest to that. As far as Satan, the enemy, is concerned, it's bad enough that we open our Bibles to listen to God. But it seems that he attacks even harder when it's time for prayer. He'll often bring anything he can to mind to try and steal our concentration. It might be something as silly as remembering we need to polish our shoes, to suddenly mentally reenacting an angry confrontation we recently experienced.

What should we pray about with our spouses? Anything and everything. Paul's words to the Thessalonians were "Pray without ceasing" (1 Thessalonians 5:17). That means developing the habit of talking with God about *everything* that's going on in our life, whether it's the frustration we're feeling about our car problems or the health of an ailing parent.

We also need to make our spouse and family a special focal point of our prayers. One of the best books I've seen in a long time is *Praying God's Will for My Wife*, by Lee Roberts. His book is nothing but Scriptures that have been personalized into prayers for a wife. (There are also books for a husband, daughter, or son.) Instead of praying for the five thousandth time, "Lord, bless my wife this morning at work and this afternoon with the kids," how about praying God's Word for her? A prayer like: "I pray that my wife will trust in You, Lord, with all her heart, and lean not on her own understanding. I pray that in all her ways she will acknowledge You, and You will direct her paths" (Proverbs 3:5–6).[2]

That's dynamite! When we pray like that for the people we love, we can know our prayers are according to the will of God—because we're praying for God's Word to be more a part of their lives.

4. Have "At Home" Worship Services

Obviously, your own church on Sunday mornings should be your primary place of worship. But on occasion, bring a "worship service" right to your home!

Worship, when boiled down to its essential element, is exactly that—acknowledging openly some attribute of God's character. God has done so much for us, we owe it to Him to speak positively about Him before others. It pleases Him, strengthens us, and encourages those who hear us about how good God is. How can you do that as a couple? Here are three ideas:

(1) Sing. Now, I know what you're thinking. "Wait a minute, Trent. When I sing, people call the police because they think I'm torturing the dog." Well, be grateful, for God is graciously tone-deaf while we're here on earth. He doesn't care if you're not Pavarotti. He's interested in your praise. The important thing is to express your appreciation to Him. It's amazing how worshipful just two people can feel singing a chorus a cappella in their living room.

(2) Read Aloud a Verse That Captures Some Element of Praise. Psalms 144 through 150 are songs of praise you can use. You can also try any number of modern-day songbooks or hymnals.

(3) Write Your Own Words of Praise. God has gifted many of us with a wonderful ability to express the way we feel through the written word. Why not buy a special notebook, entitle it "Words for My Savior," and keep things you write to Him there? They don't have to be epic poems or profound bits of prose. A few lines of praise to Him will soon yield a wealth of valuable insights and heartfelt praise that will be an eternal gift to Him and a valuable keepsake for your children.

5. Invite God to Every Dinner

I remember like it was yesterday the first time I ever

prayed in public. As a new Christian who had just moved to Texas to go to college, I soon was part of an active Young Life leadership group, helping with my guitar at a local high school. After one high school football game, a group of us leaders went out for a bite. We were all crowded around a Kip's Big Boy table, and I ordered my usual—onion rings and chocolate milk.

When our waitress brought out everyone's order, the table suddenly got quiet. I looked around, not understanding the reason, when the head Young Life leader leaned over and said, "John, would you pray for the food?"

I'd seen Norman Rockwell pictures, so I knew people prayed at dinner—but I'd always been one of the two guys at the other table staring at those people with their heads bowed. Now I was being asked to become one of them.

I took a deep breath, closed my eyes, and prayed my first prayer for the food in public. I had a warm feeling in my heart when I opened my eyes and saw everyone at the table smiling at me . . . until I looked down and saw why they were smiling.

In our Young Life leadership group, there was a tradition that I didn't know about. Namely, when you prayed for your food, you not only closed your eyes, but you covered your food with your hands as well. If not, the other people would steal your food while you prayed. Every one of my onion rings was gone—stuffed in somebody's mouth—and my chocolate milk had been drained to the last drop! I couldn't believe it!

If it's not a regular practice in your home,
I'd urge you to set a place at your table for the Savior.

In spite of the trauma of that first public prayer, it soon became a God-honoring habit. They weren't long prayers to draw attention but simple opportunities to bow my head and give thanks for God's good gifts, including the food that sustains us.

If it's not a regular practice in your home, I'd urge you to set a place at your table for the Savior. Make sure your prayers are more than just a mindlessly memorized blessing. See to it that He's as much a part of your conversation as "Pass the potatoes." After all, He's no stranger to your table; He's there every night whether you realize it or not. Treat Him as the honored guest that He is.

Even when we have non-Christian friends or family over to our house, I always explain to them that in the Trent family we take a moment to thank the Lord for the food. And then in a brief conversational way, I'll thank the Lord for the meal and for those who share it with us. Yes, it has occasionally made a guest feel uncomfortable, but that's fine with me. My prayer is that one day they'll feel comfortable enough to truly join in the praying.

We've shared many a meal with one family member in particular who doesn't know Christ (yet!). In over a decade, he's never sat down with us in public or at our house when we didn't pray. Prayer at the table has become something expected—even for him! A short time ago, we sat down in a restaurant and I got busy cutting up food for Laura (our youngest). I was so absorbed in getting her plate ready that I was startled when this family member said, "Aren't we going to pray for the food, yet?"

We all sat in stunned silence—then broke into laughter. I asked him if *he* wanted to be the one to pray, which of course he declined. But God's winning! Today he's uncomfortable if we don't pray for the food. Tomorrow we pray he'll pray to receive Christ.[3]

Solomon's bride took comfort in the fact that their home was built according to God's "building code." They had the firm foundation with their heavenly Father, and then "beams and rafters" of praise, prayer, and spiritual truth to support them. Can you say that about your relationship? A "yes" answer can go a long way toward gaining a love for all seasons.

CHAPTER 14

Principle #8
PLANNED SPONTANEITY

Every Sunday for ten years, my friend Jimmy Zorn had eleven angry and very large defensive players trying to hit him hard enough to knock him out of the game! An All-Pro quarterback for the Seattle Seahawks, he was like most players at his position: with all that "beef" bearing down on him, he was highly motivated to make decisions and act on them quickly. Jim Zorn was one of the best, a wizard at improvising and scrambling to make a long pass play. Zorn's favorite target was a player he helped put in the Hall of Fame, Steve Largent (who is now a United States congressman).

Spontaneity is important for a quarterback, and Jim brought that trait home to his wife, Joy, and their daughters as well. Yet there was one time when Jim's talent for taking charge and making quick decisions at home backfired on him.

At the time, Jim and Joy were living in a gorgeous home right on the lake in Mercer Island, near Seattle. They had a dock on their property where I actually caught my first salmon when I stayed there one night! (It was a *fingerling* salmon, but that still counts to us Arizona fishermen!)

Almost every day, they could stand in their kitchen and

watch seaplanes taking off and landing, and that's when the idea struck Jim. It was off-season, and Joy and he were long overdue to spend a weekend away. Like coming up with a touchdown play in a split second, it was suddenly clear to him. *Kidnap Joy and fly her by seaplane to an island in the middle of nowhere for the weekend!* It would be the ultimate way to "get away from it all" and be together.

Instantly, the quarterback in him sprinted into action. He started making calls, scheduling reservations, arranging for child care, and secretly packing camping gear and luggage. He was sure he had everything covered, from videos for the kids to food for the dog. This was going to be an "All-Pro" marriage weekend!

The day finally came. The prearranged baby-sitter just "happened" to be there, and he nonchalantly talked everyone into going outside and enjoying the day. With everyone out playing in the yard, their special transportation arrived right on schedule! It was a beautiful seaplane that landed on the water and then taxied right up to their dock. Naturally, the kids and the dog went crazy, and Joy was completely surprised. "Everything's taken care of," he said. "We can get away and be alone together. Come on, Joy, let's go!"

She and Jim climbed into the plane (Jim had already snuck out and loaded the luggage and camping equipment), and they took off to one of the Northwest's beautiful, secluded islands for a great weekend together. A touchdown scored for spontaneity . . . right? Think again; it was only a short pass.

Yes, it was a wonderful idea, and Joy was thrilled Jim had taken so much care and tried so hard to surprise her. But Joy (like Cindy) is a very orderly and detailed person.

After they landed at their weekend hideaway, Joy began asking question after question about whether Jim had "remembered" several important things about the kids' schedule, the things she'd planned for the weekend, and taking care of the house. For her to relax, she needed to know those important details were taken care of.

That weekend, watching Joy make call after call back to

their house, Jim learned an important "on the field" lesson in marriage—in most cases, planning doesn't kill spontaneity, it *increases* it. His was a great idea that showed his love and desire to get away with his beloved bride, but if Joy had just known a few details in advance she would have been freer to truly enjoy the moment.

I'm not saying that you can't have a surprise fortieth birthday party for your spouse or that you shouldn't spontaneously decide to go to dinner if it isn't written in ink in your Day-Timer®. But planned spontaneity has its value.

Planned spontaneity isn't a crazy contradiction, like *mild hot sauce*. It's actually our eighth and final way to nurture love. So let's look at another wise suggestion from the wife of the world's wisest man.

A PLANNED RETREAT

In Song 7, the honeymoon (described in Song 4) is over. As you might imagine, the demands on the royal family are now significant. Solomon is a "working ruler" who presides over his people in a hands-on way. He is busy judging disputes and leading the most prosperous nation of his day.

That's why his bride beckons her husband to do something for their relationship that will also bring him back refreshed and renewed to lead God's people. Namely, take a trip away from the demands of the palace to the naturally beautiful countryside where they first fell in love. In suggesting a time to rekindle their passion and keep their love strong, she says,

> "Come, my beloved, let us go out into the country,
> Let us spend the night in the villages.
> Let us rise early and go to the vineyards;
> Let us see whether the vine has budded
> and its blossoms have opened,
> And whether the pomegranates have bloomed.
> There I will give you my love." (7:11–12)

It will be a time of lovemaking, yes, but also one in

which they can reflect on the past and look forward to the future. It's an invitation to enjoy a time of "planned spontaneity" where they can renew their spirits in the midst of God's beautiful creation.

In this day and age, either you're setting your schedule, or someone else is setting it for you. If you happen to have a newborn in the house, the infant wins every conflict in the scheduling department. But in nearly all other settings (even if you are in the military, own a small business, are an "on call" medical doctor, or live on a farm), *given enough lead time and a healthy commitment,* you can add this eighth picture of love to your marriage.

GET AWAY TWICE A YEAR

Solomon's wife called upon him to "go out into the country" for a respite. I believe every couple (my wife and I included) should get away *twice a year* to renew and enrich their relationship. It's the best way to escape the breakneck pace of modern life that takes an incredible toll on relationships. What I'm suggesting is you take two weekends to "flesh out" this eighth principle of love: enrich your marriage by spending exclusive time as a twosome. Spend one weekend attending an "other-planned" event, such as a marriage or parenting conference; plan the other weekend on your own. During this second weekend I recommend you and your spouse go through the other seven pictures of love you've learned in this book.

I believe both experiences are crucial. Gaining insights from godly teachers can add tremendous tools, skills, and motivation to better love your Lord, your spouse, and your children. But you need your own custom-made weekend away as well. This second weekend leaves behind the experts and relies on the expert knowledge you have of yourselves and your unique situation, as well as on an invaluable counselor you can take with you—the Holy Spirit.

If the thought of going away for the weekend stops you short, don't worry. Shortly, I'll walk you through a plan you can personalize for a "spontaneous," well-planned weekend of your own. But first, let me give you some tips on speakers and existing seminars I know of which could be your "other-planned" weekend event.

"Other-Planned" Enrichment Opportunities

Often the best weekends are planned by a local pastor or Christian counselor at a retreat setting or church right near your home. But those listed below would certainly warrant a phone call for more information when they end up in your area. Most of these speakers hold Friday night and Saturday all-day sessions at sponsoring local churches at very reasonable cost in comparison to secular conferences. (Some do hold sessions at convention centers or hotels.) My advice is to check with your local Christian bookstore to see who's coming to town. As a wonderful source of books and music, bookstores also act as clearinghouses on Christian seminars and concerts in the area.

If at all possible, I would recommend staying at a hotel at least one night, if not both. However, if getting away to a hotel twice a year is simply not feasible due to financial or work restrictions, then I encourage you to make this "other-planned" weekend an in-town event, and make your Personal Enrichment Weekend—the one with just your spouse and you—at a hotel (or house-sitting a friend's house—more on that later).

Among the speakers I currently recommend are (in no particular order or ranking) Gary Smalley, Tim Kimmel, Steve Farrar, Jay Carty, Gary Rosberg, Tony Evans, Dennis Rainey, Howard Hendricks, Chuck Snyder, Les Parrot, and any of the speakers at Campus Crusade's Family Life Conferences.[1] There are many excellent women speakers who occasionally lead marriage retreats with their husbands. They include Florence Littauer, Barbara Johnson, Barb Snyder, Lindy Weber, Patsy Clairmont, Leslie Parrot, and Barb Rosberg.[2] These are just some of the many talented and gifted people who facilitate excellent "other-planned" enrichment weekends.

Personalized Planned Enrichment Opportunities

Then there's the *second* weekend during the year I'd encourage you to set aside to focus on your marriage. This is your own Personal Enrichment Weekend. Without a doubt, it will take more advance planning and effort than simply sending in a registration form. However, I feel it's a crucial commitment to help you pinpoint areas you *personally* need to talk about and experience blessings and insights only the two of you can find.

> *"Planned spontaneity..." is an essential part of keeping intimacy alive in the 1990s.*

Can you use this plan in a group setting? I know several church groups who have used this same plan for their couples' class retreat to combine the "best of both worlds." However, if you do, make it clearly understood that except during "free times," meals, and an occasional group service, couples are coming to spend individual time without interruption.

PLANNING A PERSONAL ENRICHMENT WEEKEND STEP BY STEP

Getting away for a weekend with a purpose is something Cindy and I have done for more than a dozen years and wouldn't trade for the world. Don't wait for the "feeling" to hit you or for the weekend to plan itself. "Planned spontaneity" means stepping out to spend quality time together, and it is an essential part of keeping intimacy alive in the 1990s. With beepers and television sets turned off, and with kids and pets well taken care of, you're able to retreat to a quiet setting and take stock of where you've been, how you're doing as a couple today, and, with prayer, where you feel God would have you and your spouse go next.

So how do you "spontaneously" plan a Personal Enrichment Weekend for just the two of you? Let me suggest the following three steps (which Cindy and I also practice). Obviously, you'll need to make specific modifications if you have six children at home or none, or if your schedule is clear enough to begin planning a month ahead, instead of six. But for the couples we meet who all seem to be living life on the dead run, this plan is tested and realistic.

Step 1: Take care of details

Six months beforehand. Pick a date for your personalized retreat. Make a commitment that, barring an emergency or serious illness, nothing will get in the way of that being your special weekend together. Your marriage deserves and needs focused time. A weekend away doesn't spell selfishness, but signals wisdom.

Start right off by setting a budget you can afford. Part of why you're starting so early is to be able to pay cash for your weekend, not increase marital stress by going into debt. Without becoming an accountant, get some general figures for lodging, meals, gas, spending money, and a small emergency fund for things unforeseen, like minor car repairs on that incredible "antique."

Don't be afraid of having to pinch a few pennies here and there to pull this off. There are dozens of ways to make a wonderful trip a low-cost one. You can even call ahead and arrange to switch houses with some good friends for the weekend. For example, ask a couple in the next town to watch your kids *at your house,* while you stay at their house for your retreat. Explain to them why you're asking this, then offer to return the favor for them on a different weekend. That way you both end up with more room than any hotel room you could afford to stay at!

Three months beforehand. Confirm the location. By this time, you should have a good idea if you're putting away enough change to stay "on budget." This is when you should call in advance reservations to a hotel or campsite. This is more necessary than you might think, even in cities that have "plenty" of hotels, and even if you've picked an off-peak weekend. It may be off-peak, but it might be the exact weekend the Royal Order of Hippos is having its convention and every room in town is booked!

Go out for dinner or ice cream and have fun with this part of the planning process. Take a map, travel brochures, etc., to plan the details of your trip. (Like the senior prom, half the fun of going is the planning and long anticipation.) Laugh, dream, discuss what you'd love to do, especially on your "free time" Saturday and Sunday afternoons. Also, make a few mental notes about your spouse's "free time" ideas in advance. Then, use those suggestions to honor each other's interests if at all possible.

Two months beforehand. Make arrangements for child care. Please don't underestimate how severely your "intimate" weekend can be torpedoed by trying to throw together child care at the last moment. Nothing can ruin a weekend faster than wondering if the kids are OK. (Making special arrangements for an aging parent will add to your emotional freedom as well.)

Two weeks beforehand. Prepare for something you'll be doing on Friday night (more to come on this later). As I suggested in the chapter on "Practicing Praise" on your spouse, pick a character trait, spiritual gift, or godly attitude that you appreciate about your loved one. Then begin putting together a special (and secret) "picture of praise" to share with him or her during dinner Friday night. (Review chapters 6 and 7 on how to do this.) Additionally, agree to spend no more than you would for a single lunch meal, on a small, tangible object to reinforce your words. (The clothespin I gave Cindy to tell her how much I appreciated her "keeping everything together" [page 70] is the kind of small item to link with your "picture of praise.") Wrap your small gift and tuck it away for the trip—but don't forget it. (Again, more on this later.)

One week before you leave. Ask a few special friends and family members to pray for your trip. Things to include in their prayers are: safety on your trip, God's protection for your children, and His blessing on your time together.

One day before you leave. Spend extra time with your children. Arrange, if at all possible, to come home from work early Thursday night. Even if you can't, try to have as much of your packing and last-minute details taken care of beforehand to allow you to spend extra time with them that night.

One important reminder: If your kids are five or older (or if they're very perceptive three or four year olds), don't make your leaving seem like a "parenthesis" in their little lives. A weekend is a long time to a child (and a necessary time for their parents). Let them know how important this time is for you to recharge your batteries and come back as a better Mommy and Daddy. Let them know *where* you're going, even showing them on a map just where you'll be each day. Ask them to pray for you, and assure them you're praying for them. *Tell them you will make one call to check in on them, one time*—like Saturday afternoon before dinner, where you can say you love and miss them. Don't call more often, *but don't forget to make the call.*

"D-Day" morning or early afternoon. The day you leave, make sure you've got your luggage, bread and grape juice for communion on Sunday (more on this later), *and a copy of this book,* which will be your enrichment plan. Then, as you drive to your hideaway, be it the Marriott, Motel 6, or Aunt Margaret's cabin, begin your weekend by asking God's blessing as you go. Thank Him for allowing you to have this special time together, and ask Him to use it to make your marriage stronger and more godly.

Step 2: *Crafting a weekend with a purpose*

You're on your way! Here's my suggestion for what to do on your weekend—but remember it's *your* weekend. The following plan is one I use with the couples I work with, and it has proven very effective. But feel free to adapt it to your unique personalities and needs as necessary.

SUGGESTED OVERALL STRUCTURE
Friday Afternoon

Side-by-Side Sharing: Discuss questions from chapters 3, 4, and 5 on "Character" on the drive up.

Check into your hotel or friend's house.

Pick a nice, quiet restaurant where you can share your "Picture of Praise" from chapters 6 and 7.

Saturday Morning

Enjoy breakfast and a short quiet time together.

Side-by-Side Sharing: Honestly look at any past "leaving" issues affecting you by discussing chapters 8 and 9.

Morning break time: have coffee or take a walk around the woods or property.

Side-by-Side Sharing: Bring up any "foxes" (chapter 10) you see that need to be dealt with, including one "take away" solution to deal with each.

Saturday Afternoon and Evening

Lunch together and afternoon free time

Evening "Dream Dinner" to talk about personal goals or dreams

"Optimal Intimacy Exercise" to end the early evening (see page 234)

Sunday Morning

Breakfast or late breakfast buffet

Couple worship service and spiritual life discussion (chapter 13)

Lunch and free time

Sunday Afternoon Drive Home

Talk about how to increase "running together" as a couple (chapter 12) and plans or places you could go for your next weekend together.

Overall goal of the weekend: To talk through the first seven pictures of love over two days in a loving, honoring way. The goal is not to solve every problem, but rather to listen and learn from your spouse. Finally, your spouse and you will decide together on several "take home" projects that can better help you grow in Christ and with each other until your next weekend together.

Two Common Questions

Before we look briefly at each major element of the weekend, let me answer two often asked questions.

1. *"We've never done something like this before. What do we talk about during these Side-by-Side sessions and discussion times?"* First, you don't have to set a record for most words exchanged in a forty-eight-hour period. However, each of these eight pictures of love can give you a great platform for couple discussion. The study guide questions at the end of this book can be a basic guide for each chapter discussion; the questions for this chapter include a commitment form to sign, as well as the "Optimal Intimacy Exercise." I also suggest a Couple's Worship Service (see "Sunday Morning" later in this chapter). In short, you've got everything you need right here to begin talking about issues and areas. Relax and have a great weekend rediscovering each other. You might be surprised how much you have to talk about!

2. *"We have trouble talking about issues without arguing here in town. What if we get out of town and have an argument?"* That might happen, but if heated words are that common in your home, then that's a clear indication you've skipped weekends like this in the past. If you're in counseling right now, I recommend you show your pastor or counselor this outline and get his or her "green light" before going away on your own. However, without exaggeration, I believe 95 percent or more of couples can gain a great deal from a weekend like this—even if they have an argument in the process.

In fact, you may even want to "schedule" an argument during the "foxes" discussion time. Then talk about what happened, how you handled things, and what you could do differently. I've often had couples tell me that the most difficult part of the weekend was the most rewarding. When you are finally ready to head out the door, read carefully and sign in front of your spouse your Couple Commitment Card in the study guide (page 233).

Specific Events at Your Personal Enrichment Weekend

Your enrichment sessions begin the moment you drive out of your driveway! As mentioned, you've already got the handbook for your weekend right in your hand—this book. On your way to your destination, use this time away from the phone (even cellular phones) to talk about chapters 3 and 4 on *character*.

Whoever isn't driving can lead a discussion through the study questions at the end of this book. Even if you've gone through them already, they can be a good review to see what character issues you've worked on, or if any still present a problem and why. In all your discussion, if your spouse sees an area you could work on, or offers advice on how to improve, *don't see it as a criticism*. View it as an *opportunity* to become even better at your marriage. In fact, I've found that Cindy is often *more attracted* to me when I'm willing to admit a fault and be serious about improving it, rather than trying to defend myself. None of us is perfect—we never will be (at least, not this side of heaven). Be quick to praise, but be honest if there are growth issues to discuss as well. One key to intimacy that Solomon and his bride had was the ability to be open and vulnerable with each other. Give your spouse that same gift.

Friday Evening. After you arrive and settle in, have a nice dinner together (either cook together or go out to eat). During dessert, share your "praise pictures" with each other, and give your spouse the small item you've chosen to illustrate it.

This is also a great time to relive some of the memorable moments of your courtship. Remember that Solomon's wife saw the value in returning to the place where they first fell in love to rekindle that love. You can do that at the dinner table tonight by simply taking time to relive those memories together. This is also a great time to share why you first fell in love with each other.

Saturday Morning. You'll have two sessions this morning, and you'll need to be alert, so enjoy a great breakfast together first. Then, in your first session, discuss the whole issue of *leaving home.* To do that, review the four "Steps in Leaving Home" in chapters 8 and 9. Then discuss these questions with each other: Have I successfully worked through this? Has my spouse? If we haven't, what can we do to take care of the issue right now?

If you need more information, read the portion of chapter 8 or 9 that pertains to the issue you're thinking about. If there are issues you still need to deal with, decide together on the best strategy for overcoming them and *write that plan down. Remember, your goal isn't to solve everything.* By the time you get home, you will have prayed over a list of things that you can begin to work on until next year's enrichment retreat. You can't bring closure to every issue in one weekend, but you can begin the process and triple the level of hope and motivation to change growth areas that remain.

Spend at least forty minutes together talking about these "family background" issues but not more than an hour and a half without taking your morning break. If some issues remain unresolved, again write them down and promise to begin working on them when you get home.

During your break, get out of the room. Walk in the woods or along the beach, jump in the swimming pool, or run around the block. That way you'll be more refreshed and ready to go for the next session.

Saturday Late Morning. Now you're ready for session two, which deals with chasing those "foxes" that may be ruining your vineyard. During this session, you'll want to accomplish two things: First, take a look at the portion of chapter 10 called "How to Let Little Foxes Become Strong Predators." Take each of the things listed there and ask these questions together: Do we see any of these things becoming a habit in our relationship? Which ones? Is there a seventh "fox" we're facing?

Second, once you've identified those things that could turn into predators in your relationship, turn to the section of chapter 10 called "Fox Hunting" and follow the steps there for hunting down each "fox."

The last two parts of that plan require that you follow up

with each other over the next few months, so don't let that slip. I suggest each of you keep a notebook nearby to write down your thoughts and record areas you can focus on when you get home. Again, like the first session, spend no less than forty minutes but no more than an hour and a half on this discussion as well.

Saturday Afternoon. Around noon, break for lunch. Then you've got the rest of the afternoon to do whatever you'd like—except continuing to discuss Friday evening's or Saturday morning's issues. Many issues may be too big to reach closure in forty to ninety minutes; you still should plan fun time together. Stop at the end of your discussion time, *pray together,* and then head out for lunch and some recreation. For you, that may be going shopping, taking in a movie, or going for a walk—whatever you enjoy.

Saturday Evening. Plan a special dinner celebration together. (This time, eat at a restaurant if at all possible.) Remember, it doesn't have to be fancy to be memorable. One of those nice buffet places can offer just as much as a fancy restaurant where waiters put your napkin in your lap. (And I guarantee you the portions will be bigger at the buffet!)

During this dinner, talk about some personal plans you have. Perhaps it's that dream of going back and finishing your college degree. Or changing careers if you had the opportunity, or moving to Kodiak, Alaska, every summer when the salmon are running. Give yourself and your spouse the freedom to discuss "dreams" at this dinner without the pressure to turn them into action when you get home. In other words, no announcing at dinner, "Honey . . . guess where we're moving next week!" Instead, share from the heart, without criticism or having to bring closure, some personal dreams you have. If you need to, start the ball rolling by asking each other, "If you knew you had three months to live, what would you do and where would you go?"

If you've noticed that I've stressed not having to bring closure to each issue you discuss, you're very observant. Go back to the goal of this weekend. It's not to try and make up for daily or weekly interaction that's been neglected for ten years in one weekend. That's a certain setup for failure. The goal of this time is to get you hooked on being together in a special way, and to identify enrichment areas you can work on when you get back in the real world until your next retreat together.

Saturday Night. After dinner, a quiet stroll in a peaceful setting (or going to an ice cream place for dessert) might be a great way to wind down the evening. When you return to your room, here are a couple of suggestions to conclude the night. First, don't put pressure on yourself to "end" this evening with lovemaking. If you'll remember from chapter 11, first thing in the *morning* is often a time of even greater arousal. If you both want to be intimate this evening, that's wonderful. If not, that's wonderful too! *Sometime during the weekend,* as Solomon's bride suggests, enjoying sexual intimacy is important. Plan that "spontaneous" time if it's helpful. But don't seek to pressure the other person into record-setting sexual activity.

In fact, you might even want (on Friday or Saturday night) to include the "Intimacy Exercise" (on page 234) that asks couples *not* to have intercourse during the experience and for half an hour afterward. This is an exercise I learned in a doctoral class and have given as a "honeymoon" assignment to many couples. It's also a great "refresher course" on intimacy for us slightly older married folks.

The point of the exercise is to create an atmosphere in which you and your spouse feel free to express your love in a God-honoring way. If you feel there are issues you need to talk about when it comes to intimacy, don't try and discuss them before or during the intimacy exercise. Rather, include that as part of the "foxes" discussion in the early morning where it can be talked about when you're fresh and free from evening expectations. Remember, you can review the sections in chapter 11 called "Three Common Misconceptions to Avoid" and "Six Ways to Nourish a Positive Sexual Response." You may decide—after the weekend and when you get back home—to purchase Tim and Beverly LaHaye's *The Act of Marriage* or Ed Wheat's *Intended for Pleasure*, which gives much more detailed information and insights on sex in marriage.

Sunday Morning. After breakfast, you should spend time focusing on your spiritual life together. If you're like most couples, this can be one of the most fulfilling and rewarding parts of the whole weekend. I recommend you design your own "Couple's Worship Service" ahead of time, complete with music, worship, and sharing God's Word. Bring a song sheet or personal hymnal, and each of you pick a favorite hymn you can sing a cappella. Read Psalm 103 as an act of worship and as a responsive reading where one person reads one verse, and the other the next. This psalm lists a number of traits our heavenly Father displays, each of which is worthy of our worship and praise. Bring a cassette tape of your pastor or one of your favorite speakers, or each of you pick a passage of Scripture ahead of time that you feel brings special bearing to your present circumstances. (For example, if you're facing a move, read Joshua 1:1–9, where God assures Joshua repeatedly that He will be with him wherever he goes.)

Close your time together by sharing Communion (unless, of course, that violates your tradition). Before you do, choose one of the following passages on God's love for you and read it aloud together: Isaiah 40 or Romans 8:31–39. Then, take the elements together. As you do, read one of the following passages that talks about Communion at the Last Supper: Matthew 26:26–30, Mark 14:22–26, Luke 22:14–20, or 1 Corinthians 11:23–29. What a marvelous way to wrap up your worship service!

The Drive Home. You can depart after lunch and whatever free time you include before you decide to get back into the real world. On your way home, you have one last task. That's to look at where you are as a leadership team and what you can do to be even more effective at "running together" this next year. This can include a discussion of chapter 13 if you like. In addition, take out your notebooks and make sure you have written down the areas or goals you've set to work on when you get back. As you're driving, prioritize the list, and even bring along your calendar to see when you could set discussion times if needed.

Step 3: One last look back

As you near home, take a few moments to reflect on the last couple of days. Share what you've learned, how you feel, any fears you have, etc. Then, stop the car at a local park or quiet area close to your house. Now that you're back in familiar surroundings, pray for the things you've talked about. Ask for God's guidance and counsel, for His wisdom and strength. Ask Him to help you remember lessons learned and to keep you from allowing the everyday to swallow the significant.

Pray for each of your children you're about to see, and for their future spouses, and for their children. Finally, thank Him for allowing you an opportunity to get away and reflect. Rededicate yourselves to His design for your marriage and to growing closer to Him and each other as you practice these eight steps to intimacy.

CHAPTER 15

LASTING LOVE: A FINAL LOOK

Solomon and his bride made their relationship beautiful by following the eight principles in this book. Together they adorned their marriage with eight pictures of love, and you can too. As we close, let me display one final picture of a couple who put all eight of these principles into practice, and the difference it made in their lives.

Unlike Solomon, George grew up a pauper in incredibly trying circumstances. In his tiny home in Detroit, his parents fought constantly and his two older brothers were deaf. One of George's earliest memories was of asking his mother something at the dinner table only to have his father look at him in anger and say, "You're not deaf!"

THE GO-BETWEEN

George learned sign language at the same time he learned to speak, and soon he became the "go-between" between his parents and two very angry brothers. He also became the designated "stand-between" person who had to break up fights between his parents (including one evening when his mother picked up a butcher knife with deadly intent to use it).

With all that hurt, George became a teenager who raced

cars and ran with a rough crowd. But one day he was swept off his feet by a lovely young lady. Darlene had that Maureen O'Hara spunk and confidence, complete with the fiery red hair. Unlike George, she came from a close-knit home, where her father was in many ways her closest friend.

George was smitten, and soon so was Darlene. They married and lived happily ever after—that is, *after* they came to know Jesus Christ. Until then, their marriage faced major challenges, especially in the area of communication. George knew how to be silent and withdrawn (like his brothers), while Darlene wanted communication and closeness. Though they were blessed with two beautiful girls, things came together only when they began to let the Lord lead their lives.

George and Darlene have spent years practicing these eight ways to intimacy. They've looked at the pictures of love modeled in Song of Songs, and they've spent years working at reflecting them. From praise to character building, to capturing "foxes," to dealing with past issues, they've studied each picture and asked God to redraw it onto the fabric of their own marriage. And it's worked. They also have included Personal Enrichment Weekends in their schedules for years, and they have found that the weekends have greatly helped their communication and understanding of each other.

George and his wife now have a love that is a model for many others, including the dozens of premarital couples they have worked with over the years. Young couples see real people as they watch George, an auto body repairman, and Darlene, a wife who operates a small catering business. George and Darlene are honest about their struggles, but totally committed to their Savior.

SILENT NIGHT . . . HOLY NIGHT

In George's early life, the words "Silent Night" did not represent a song; it was how he lived. If he wasn't sharing the silent world of his two older brothers, he was looking desperately for a "silent" place to hide when his parents were fighting. But that pattern hasn't transferred down to his home. He and Darlene can sing "Silent night, holy night" because they've continued to look to Christ.

They've looked at another picture of love found on a hill far away, not in Solomon's palace. It's the picture of a cross and of nail-scarred hands, a picture of a risen Christ with the power to transform who they were into all He wants them to become. It's a picture of love I hope you have hanging in your heart, of a Savior who loved you enough to lay down His life and make it possible for you to have eternal life.

In truth, it is Christ's love, reflected so well through Solomon and his bride, that we've been looking at all this time. And it's His love that will maintain and sustain you through every new season of life. That, my friends, is my most fervent prayer for you.

YOUR PLACE ALONG THE WAY

Where are you along the way toward deeper intimacy in your marriage? After looking at these eight principles for developing a lasting love, depicted in eight vivid pictures of Solomon and his bride, you may feel that you are moving along the path, have just taken a few steps, or are completely lost. To get an accurate measurement of where you are (and where you need to go) in nurturing intimacy in your relationship, complete the following inventory. It can help you look beyond your feelings and recognize where you and your spouse are in attitudes and actions. And it can be a springboard to discussion and change. (The numbers in parentheses indicate the chapter where the principle is discussed.)

So (gently) grab your spouse and sit down together with the following inventory. Then, based on your findings, chart a new course, working especially on those areas where you score the lowest. Complete the inventory again about six months later to chart your progress and perhaps to make a midcourse change of direction. May you gain a deeper love for your spouse as you follow these eight ways to greater intimacy.

INTIMACY INVENTORY

Answer the following questions by circling the appropriate number. (Remember, the number in parentheses refers to the chapter where the principle is discussed.)

1. If those who know you well were asked to describe the purity of your character, would they say it's more like axle grease or virgin olive oil? (3)

Axle grease   *Virgin olive oil*

   1   2   3   4   5   6   7

2. How would you rate the consistency of your individual devotional life? (13)

Inconsistent   *Consistent*

(less than   (at least five times
once per week)   per week)

   1   2   3   4   5   6   7

3. How successful have you been in severing the tie to your parents and bonding with your spouse (i.e., "leaving home")? (8–9)

Not successful   *Very successful*

   1   2   3   4   5   6   7

4. When was the last time you and your spouse got away together to renew your marriage? (14)

We've never done that   *Within the last six months*

   1   2   3   4   5   6   7

5. If the praise you give your spouse could be rated by volume level setting, what number on the dial would it be set at? (6)

Faint praise   *High decibel praise*

   1   2   3   4   5   6   7

6. My level of sexual satisfaction in our relationship is . . . (11)

Not satisfied   *Very satisfied*

   1   2   3   4   5   6   7

7. How good are you and your spouse at spotting problems in your relationship? (10)

Not good at all   *Very good*

   1   2   3   4   5   6   7

8. How skilled are you and your spouse at solving problems you see? (10)

Not skilled   *Very skilled*

   1   2   3   4   5   6   7

9. If your partnership in the home were compared to riding a bicycle built for two, would you say . . . (12)

We never   *We usually*
pedal together   *pedal together*

   1   2   3   4   5   6   7

10. How secure do you feel in your relationship with your spouse? (12)

Not very secure   *Very secure*

   1   2   3   4   5   6   7

11. If *60 Minutes* filmed everything you did and said during one day of your life, how pleased would you be to have it broadcast on Sunday night? (5)

Not pleased   *Ready to call*
at all   *my friends/relatives*

   1   2   3   4   5   6   7

12. How freely are you able to enjoy sex with your spouse? (11)

Not freely   *Very freely*

    1   2   3   4   5   6   7

13. When you need advice on an important decision, are you more likely to seek the advice of your parents or of your spouse? (8)

My parents   *My spouse*

    1   2   3   4   5   6   7

14. If you asked my spouse how well I fulfill my role as a husband/wife, he/she would say I . . . (12)

Need a good deal   *Am doing a*
of work   *good job*

    1   2   3   4   5   6   7

15. When it comes to getting away with my spouse on a marriage retreat . . . (14)

I'm not sure I   *I'm committed*
can make time   *to making time*

    1   2   3   4   5   6   7

16. Our devotional life together as a couple reminds me of . . . (13)

An old car   *An F-16 jet*

(it's hard to start and   (it's powerful and
doesn't run very well)   soars to new heights)

    1   2   3   4   5   6   7

RECORDING THE RESULTS

Add the numbers you circled and enter the total here: _____

Mark your total score on the scale below:

Low intimacy   *High intimacy*

16   35   55   85   112

Date: _____

If you scored 112, then you're probably living on the second moon of the planet Zadar. But for those of us who are on earth (and are honest in taking tests like these), don't get discouraged whatever your score is. If it's high, that's great! Keep up the good work. If it shows you need work, then it simply means you have some exciting things to discover and incorporate into your relationship that will make it more intimate and deep than you thought possible.

So, put your arm around your spouse, look him or her in the eye, and together pray and commit before God to do whatever it takes to make your relationship rich, warm, loving, and secure. You *can* learn to live out these eight principles of a lasting love.

Then I encourage you to date your score above. Six months from now retake the test and enter the results on the scale below. Compare the two to see how much your intimacy has grown.

APPLICATION PROJECT

Low intimacy   *High intimacy*

16   35   55   85   112

Date: _____

NOTES

Chapter 2: A Picture of Something Great

1. Recording from "Ministry Essentials," by Charles Swindoll, Ministry Essentials Conference, 1994, Dallas Theological Seminary.

2. We get a hint of this power for positive change when the Lord instructs a woman with an unwilling husband to model godly behavior "without a word" by her chaste and loving behavior (1 Peter 3:1–2). Remember, a spouse may explain away your words. But he or she cannot explain away your actions.

Chapter 3: A Purified Character

1. Some women may not appreciate being likened to a car, but his wife did. She knew exactly what he meant, and it made her feel more secure and loved.

2. Cindy's name still does! I have a policy here at work that no matter what work project, meeting, or counseling session I'm in, when Cindy calls—the call goes right through. She never abuses that arrangement, but I want her to know that her "name" carries weight.

3. Among those factors that can affect a spouse's level of responsiveness are physical illness, work stress, hormonal changes during or after pregnancy, and rearing toddlers and teenagers. However, clinical studies on "low sexual desire"—the term used today for the condition once called "frigidity"—recommend developing security and trust as a primary treatment goal.

4. The *long* course can be found in an entire book I wrote on developing godly character with my good friend Rick Hicks, called *Seeking Solid Ground* (Colorado Springs: Focus on the Family, 1995).

Chapter 4: The Foundation of Your Character

1. This course is very effective, and I would recommend that every Christian-owned or -operated company in the country adopt it. For information on Bill Nix's program on teaching values in the everyday workplace, write us at Encouraging Words, 12629 N. Tatum, Suite 208, Phoenix, AZ 85032.

2. Four passages I highly recommend are the Sermon on the Mount (especially the Beatitudes), Psalm 15, Deuteronomy 21, where the Ten Commandments are listed, and any passage in the New Testament that chronicles the life of Christ.

3. That's exactly what happened with two good friends of ours, Gary and Barb Rosberg. (Gary now is the president of CrossTrainers and the author of an excellent book for men called *Guard Your Heart*.) At the time, Gary couldn't comprehend why Barb would end their relationship just because he didn't know Christ. But her response was just one step in a series of events that made clear to him the reality of God's presence and love. He wrestled with committing his life to Christ, and finally did. Now they are one of the most loving and committed couples I know.

Chapter 5: Character Development

1. For a close look at this unhealthy bent toward inner duplicity, see the chap-

ter "Image Management vs. Authentic Living," in John Trent, *LifeMapping* (Colorado Springs: Focus on the Family, 1994).

Chapter 6: Practicing Praise

1. Robert Hoffman, "Recent Research on Figurative Language," *Annals of the New York Academy of Sciences* (December 1984): 137–66; Louie S. Karpress and Ming Singer, "Communicative Competence," *Psychology Reports* 59 (1986): 1299–306.

Chapter 7: Praise Lessons from a Pro

1. Actually, studies have shown that people like friends or even strangers who praise them—even when they know the person is not telling the truth. For example, salesmen who would say things like, "This has got to be your sister, not your mother!" were rated more highly in exit interviews than salesmen who didn't praise the customer. (See Helen Kelly, "The Process of Causal Attribution," *American Psychologist* 28 [1973]: 107–28.) This tendency doesn't mean people want to hear false flattery; rather it shows how much people want and positively respond to praise.

2. For an extended discussion of how the dove was used in biblical times, see "Dove," *The International Standard Bible Encyclopedia,* vol. 2, James Orr, gen. ed. (Grand Rapids: Eerdmans, 1983).

3. For 101 word pictures you can use in your home, office, or with your children, see the book Gary Smalley and I wrote, *The Language of Love* (Colorado Springs: Focus on the Family, 1989).

Chapter 8: Leaving Home

1. The "lions" and "leopards" may be poetic references to the treatment she received from the "angry brothers" we've seen earlier.

2. D. J. Owens, "The Social Structure of Violence in Childhood," *Aggressive Behavior* 12 (1975): 68.

3. For those dealing with the trauma and pain of physical and sexual abuse, I recommend two biblically based resources, *The Missing Part*, by Lee Ezell, and *The Wounded Heart*, by Dan Allender.

4. If the problems you're facing are significant enough, please consider seeking counsel from your pastor or a biblically centered counselor.

    In addition, commit yourself to "going to school," reading and seeking to apply the wisdom of four books. I recommend the following order to those I counsel in leaving home emotionally: (1) *The Blessing*, Gary Smalley and John Trent (Colorado Springs: NavPress, 1988), which asks if you received your parents' "blessing," and how you can move away from that hurt if you didn't. (Male readers may also want to read *The Hidden Value of a Man*, Gary Smalley and John Trent, for insight on overcoming a lack of positive male role-modeling); (2) *Seeking Solid Ground*, John Trent, which helps you to anchor your life "today" on a plan for godly character found in Psalm 15; (3) *LifeMapping*, John Trent, which helps in developing a clear plan for a positive future; and (4) *Intimate Moments with the Savior*, Ken Gire (Grand Rapids: Zondervan, 1989), which helps the reader to continue his/her walk away from this hurt day by day by focusing on loving and becoming like Christ.

Finally, we'll spend the bulk of a later chapter talking about the power and need for loving support and accountability, which is another key to overcoming past hurts.

Chapter 9: Walking Toward Closeness

1. In a few very important cases, we see relationships that are both complementary and symmetrical, such as in our relationship with Christ. Christ is the King of Kings and Lord of Lords, and in our relationship we worship and praise Him; He commands and deserves our loyalty and love. That's a symmetrical relationship if there ever was one! Yet it's more than that. Without losing His authority over our lives, He invites us to add a dimension to our relationship that non-believers can't experience. We have a "side by side" complementary relationship as well! The Lord of Lords invites us to pray, "Abba, Father." He tells us we've been "adopted as sons." He's gone to great lengths to prepare a place for us where we can dwell with Him forever. That's a complementary relationship if there ever was one!

2. Gordon Dalbey, *Healing the Masculine Soul* (Waco, Tex.: Word, 1988), 50–52.

3. For an extended look at these important "boundary" issues, see John Townsend and Robert Cloud, *Boundaries* (Grand Rapids: Zondervan, 1992).

Chapter 10: Chasing the Predators

1. And I think she would have liked Aunt Dovie! My precious, godly aunt passed away several years ago, but along with my mother and grandmother, she helped raise me. I used an elaborated version of this story to praise her incredible attention to detail in *The Two Sides of Love* (Pamona, Calif.: Focus on the Family, 1990), 58, when I talk about "Beavers" (or detail people).

2. Facial expressions are part of a group of mannerisms that comprise what is called *nonverbal communication*. Like tone of voice, our "nonverbals" can help or undermine our very words. Whether it is the rolling of eyes, the arching of an eyebrow, or hands on hips (to name just a few physical movements), we can convey criticism, sarcasm, and a variety of other meanings that are at odds with our message. In fact, Alan Mehrebian of Stanford University found in one study that actual words communicated only 7 percent of the message; listeners picked up 93 percent of the meaning from both the tone of voice and nonverbals (*Silent Message,* 2nd ed. [Belmont, Calif: Wadsworth, 1981]). Clearly dishonoring gestures or mannerisms are as dangerous as any of the other predators.

Chapter 11: Enjoying Physical Intimacy

1. For those who come to marriage after losing their sexual purity, that garden can be restored, as one man told his fiancée during premarital counseling. In a wonderful act of love and maturity, the husband-to-be told her, "You're forgetting something, sweetheart. The gate to your garden may have been knocked down and the flowers pulled up—but you're forgetting someone. That's the Master Gardener, Jesus Christ. He forgave the woman at the well and the woman caught in the very act of adultery. If He could forgive them and restore and replant their 'garden,' He can do the same for you." He eloquently pictured a truth that some readers need to appropriate if they're feeling guilt over past sexual sin. The Master Gardener can forgive and restore so that our garden is beautiful once again.

2. S. Craig Glickman, *A Song for Lovers* (Downers Grove, Ill.: InterVarsity, 1978), 25.

3. The Scriptures in the strongest terms warn against immorality, which can include pornography. Here are several of those verses: Leviticus 20:14; Acts 15:20; 1 Corinthians 6:13, 18; Galatians 5:19; Ephesians 5:3; and 1 Thessalonians 4:3. If nothing else, how could this minister get past the direct words of Christ to avoid wandering eyes? "You have heard it said, 'You shall not commit adultery,' but I say to you, that everyone who looks on a woman to lust for her has committed adultery with her already in his heart" (Matthew 5:27).

4. David Larsen and Marianne Herring, "Believe, Well, Live Well," *Focus on the Family*, September 1994, 2–4. The most surprising finding was that religious women reported more orgasmic responses than did nonreligious women.

5. Richard B. Stuart, "Operant Interpersonal Treatment for Marital Discord," *Journal of Consulting and Clinical Psychology* 33 (1969): 675–82.

6. A new book I recommend as well is Robert Barnes, *Great Sexpectations* (Grand Rapids: Zondervan, 1995). It is a thoroughly biblical look at the subject of sexual intimacy and well worth reading.

Chapter 12: Leadership That Draws Two Together

1. On a recent plane trip I had an opportunity to speak with a Washington lobbyist for women's rights. When I read her this passage and others out of Song of Songs, she was stunned that the Bible could be so relevant—and so honoring to women!

2. If you're a man struggling with taking the lead in a positive way, I recommend three books that can help you meet this crucial responsibility: *Tender Warrior*, by Stu Weber; *Point Man*, by Steve Farrar; and *The Hidden Value of a Man*, by Gary Smalley and John Trent.

3. Marvin Allen with Joe Robinson, *Angry Men, Passive Men* (New York: Fawcett Columbine, 1994), 32–33.

4. Warren Bennis, *On Becoming a Leader* (New York: Addison-Wesley, 1989).

5. Allen, *Angry Men*, 157.

6. To see the proper perspective in action in the lives of two Old Testament characters, study the book of Ruth and Genesis 37–45, looking at Joseph. Ruth had lost her husband and all visible means of support, but instead of feeling bitter toward God, she committed herself to her heavenly Father and to helping her mother-in-law. God rewarded her faith with a loving family. Meanwhile Joseph was sold into slavery by his brothers, falsely accused of rape and thrown into jail, and even deserted by friends who could have helped his case and gotten him released. Yet even when he finally met his brothers after years had passed, he wasn't bitter . . . but brokenhearted over their sin. He understood that their hardness of heart in wanting to hurt him was a reflection of *their* pathology, not his failing as a person. His spiritual and emotional health was apparent in the way he viewed himself as having great value to God independent of his circumstances, and in how he responded to his brothers face-to-face.

7. Carol Heilbrun, as quoted in Christina Hoff Sommers, *Who Stole Feminism?* (New York: Touchstone, 1994), cover.

8. Christina Hoff Sommers, *Who Stole Feminism?*, p. 21.

9. Marilyn French, as quoted in ibid., 43.

Chapter 13: Building Your Life According to Code

1. Bryan Knowles, "Job Versus Family: Striking a Balance," *Focus on the Family*, 19 June 1991, 2–4.

2. Lee Roberts, *Praying God's Will for My Wife* (Nashville: Nelson, 1993), 23.

3. If you're a prayer warrior, his name is George, and pray along with us for his salvation!

Chapter 14: Planned Spontaneity

1. Of course, this author also schedules and speaks at conferences across the country. If you'd like a listing of seminar cities, or if you'd like to schedule a conference for your church or city, please call or write us at Encouraging Words, 12629 N. Tatum Blvd., Suite 208, Phoenix, Arizona 85032, 1-602-922-8640.

2. Sorry! While Cindy Trent could be an outstanding women's conference speaker, she's not doing them until the kids get older. Occasionally, she joins me on the platform at a camp or conference, and people love her. Lord willing, when our daughters are older, we'll team up on many more speaking engagements.

THE LOVE FOR ALL SEASONS
STUDY GUIDE
*For Individual, Couple,
and Group Study*

by

JAMES S. BELL, JR.

INTRODUCTION

The following study guide is where the real work begins. It's time to turn the corner, as we move from insights to application. It's in putting these principles into practice that your intimacy level with your spouse will grow. Just as Solomon went well beyond good intentions to be a successful lover, so must you.

Individuals and couples have different needs and circumstances, and all the following questions may not equally apply. Each question is written to the individual, most likely married or perhaps contemplating marriage, but all the material is better utilized by couples or small groups.

Don't feel guilty if answering each question seems threatening or even overwhelming. After reading the book try to work on as many questions in each chapter as possible to keep the process moving. You don't want to get bogged down and fail to work your way to the final set of questions.

For various reasons, your husband or wife may decide not to either read the book or use the study guide. Don't let this deter you. If you take the first step to grow and change, your mate will immediately benefit, and that can only bring you closer together.

Nothing is more important in marriage than a growing, vibrant relationship with your partner. Do whatever it takes to get quiet, uninterrupted time to concentrate. It's worth your best efforts.

CHAPTER ONE

FINDING A LOVE FOR ALL SEASONS

KEY THOUGHT

Love goes beyond mere feelings. There is a set of biblical criteria that provides a standard to judge true, enduring love. There is also a vivid picture of "love in action" that helps us get beyond the confusion over our changing feelings toward our spouse.

1. Bill and Susan have experienced some of the pressures and failures in life. What negative developments—personal appearance, job tensions, communication failure, etc.—have put distance between you and your mate?

2. Brenda's concerns about love are echoed by many. What were your questions during courtship concerning the nature of love? How have those questions been answered, or how has your definition of love changed?

3. What was the one major concern or doubt you had during courtship concerning a lasting love relationship? How has that been dealt with during the course of your marriage?

4. What actions by your mate have affected you deeply? Share with one another some "pictures" of love that you have received in the past.

5. Fleeting attraction and true love can appear similar. Name two characteristics that made your initial relationship with your mate different from previous dating partners.

CHAPTER TWO

A PICTURE OF SOMETHING GREAT

KEY THOUGHT

The Song of Songs is the ultimate love story. It's a clear picture of what an ideal courtship and marriage should be. It deals with passion, leadership, praise, independence, dangers, union, proper foundations, and spontaneity.

Before you read on and discover the truths and applications behind the eight ways to greater intimacy, briefly rate your past and present performance in the eight areas this book will explore. Use the following scale:
1=Not at all, 2=Poor, 3=Average, 4=Above average, 5=Excellent

1. Your consistency in character fostering a romantic, passion-filled atmosphere with your mate. _____

2. How you exercise leadership, servanthood, and working together toward balancing each other's strengths and weaknesses. _____

3. How you build up your mate through encouragement and praise. _____

4. How you have broken away from unhealthy dependence on parents or other adults. _____

5. Absence of character flaws, attitudes, or actions that hinder intimacy. _____

6. The degree to which your sex life has hindered intimacy.
   ____

7. A strong Christian foundation and building materials based on the Bible (including spiritual disciplines). ____

8. How well you have spontaneously planned events with romantic associations. ____

Finally, name the one book or film that is your favorite love story. What attracts you, especially in terms of your own relationship?

CHAPTER THREE

A PURIFIED
CHARACTER

KEY THOUGHT

The complete integrity of the person you love is an important component of a healthy marriage; it even fuels physical desire for your spouse. A good name builds the trust and admiration necessary for physical intimacy.

1. If integrity provides the building blocks of a great marriage, compare lists of positive character traits and actions with your mate that have contributed to intimacy.

2. We may not often link deficiencies in godly character with decreasing sexual attraction, but there is a connection. What past conduct has cooled your sexual ardor, even for a short time?

3. Make a list of all the positive character traits that you consider to be your strong points. Then list the qualities that you most need to work on.

4. Integrity is tested the most in pressure situations. Consider a stressful situation in the last year where you were severely tempted or attacked yet overcame the temptation (or attack). Then consider another situation where you failed. What lessons can you learn from both the successful response and the failure? Then apply these lessons to future situations to preserve integrity.

5. Write a letter to your mate and describe what makes him/her sexually attractive *apart* from the purely sensual or fleshly elements. Try to express what enhances his or her sexuality in terms of your spouse's emotional, behavioral, or even spiritual actions.

CHAPTER FOUR

THE FOUNDATION OF YOUR CHARACTER

KEY THOUGHT

Unless Jesus Christ has become the cornerstone of the marriage relationship, the many positive character traits necessary for true intimacy will not be realized.

1. Choose one of the four Gospels to study Jesus' character. Look at three incidents in the gospel in which Jesus displayed strong character in difficult situations. Then consider how these responses could apply to your life.

2. Godly character can affect our physical lives in a positive way. How has integrity improved your own physical and emotional life, as well as your spiritual life?

3. The Bible says not to be "unequally yoked." Think about various marriages, business partnerships, etc., that you know, where even a common vision in the beginning led to strife. What character issues were at stake?

4. In what areas of your personal life is Jesus Christ firmly entrenched as the cornerstone and Lord? In what areas is the control more in your own hands?

5. As you look at your own marriage, in what key areas is Christ at the center—of your devotion, decisions, motivations, etc.? In what areas have you consciously or unconsciously deviated in your own direction?

CHAPTER FIVE

CHARACTER DEVELOPMENT: TWO STEPS FORWARD, TWO STEPS BACK

KEY THOUGHT

Our inner life as well as our outer life, our thoughts as well as our choices, must be consistent with God's standards. God's presence, in the form of His blessing and guidance, will be with us if Christ is our foundation.

1. Begin with "clean hands" and examine the visible actions, words, and attitudes you display to others. Be completely honest and objective, and list all the instances in the last month where you were less than Christlike, "cutting corners" or mistreating others in some way.

2. Now look at a "pure heart" and consider how certain external behavior may be acceptable but the thoughts and intentions behind it are not. In what areas are your concerns related more to social approval than biblical standards of the heart? Examine why there is a division and how you can choose to please God rather than yourself or others.

3. The Word of God penetrates to the thoughts and intents of our hearts and cleanses us if we submit to it. Choose three commands that touch on Christian character that you find difficult. Ask God to allow His Word to do its work.

4. One way for the Word to penetrate our lives is to be accountable to others regarding its commands. Pick someone you trust who is a mature Christian (apart from your mate) to share your struggles and performance in these critical areas. Ask that person to counsel and pray with you.

5. Besides clean hands and a pure heart, two other principles are essential for godly character. Many of us are deceived by the lies, or falsehood, of the world due to our own greed or selfishness. We also may not be faithful to our pledged commitments or promises. Truth and our word of honor should be our standard. Search out the weaknesses in these areas and seek God to correct them.

CHAPTER SIX

PRACTICING PRAISE

KEY THOUGHT

Praising our mate with creative word pictures is a very effective way of building confidence, self-assurance, and security.

1. All of us have insecurities, either based on real weaknesses or comparison to others. Be open with your spouse about your own shortcomings or inadequacies. Be prepared for feedback that is both reassuring and challenging.

2. You may (or may not) be aware of your spouse's perceived insecurities. If your mate is willing, allow him or her to share those feelings. Then express how valuable he or she is to you with a word picture, even a basic one.

3. Enjoy a romantic evening and have fun finding modern counterparts to the type of word pictures Solomon and his bride used. Why would some be inappropriate? Based on the personality type of your mate and his or her interests, seek to come up with more illustrations in light of modern day values.

4. Think again of John's clothespin story. Have you ever been surprised by a small gesture by your mate that was more meaningful than larger or more expensive acts of love? Why was it meaningful? As you recall its impact, ask yourself how you can apply this principle to your spouse in the future.

5. The greatest way to relieve our insecurities is to study the word pictures given to us by Jesus Christ concerning His steadfast love for each of us. Go beyond the four listed in the chapter and find three more. See yourself as the object of that heartfelt expression of love and protection.

CHAPTER SEVEN

PRAISE LESSONS FROM A PRO

KEY THOUGHT

If couples make a habit of praising each other's good qualities, they can put the past behind and build a more purposeful future. In this chapter we'll go beyond review to application with a practical exercise.

EXERCISE

LINKING YOUR PRAISE WITH A PICTURE

1. Pick one character trait you appreciate about your spouse. (For example, he or she is detailed, spontaneous, caring, forward thinking, honest, patient, forthright, or peaceful.) Be specific, and if your spouse is doing this exercise with you, come up with something quick!

2. With the specific trait in mind, pick one of Solomon's three categories to "picture" that trait.

a. Animals in nature

   For example, if your husband follows through on tasks around the house, he may be like a beaver who never stops working until his dam is built.

   Animal: _____
   Why did you choose it?

b. Everyday objects

For example, if you appreciate your spouse's discernment, you might pick an object like an airport security gate. "Honey," you could say, "you know when you walk through those metal detectors at the airport and the beeper sounds if someone is carrying a suspicious object? I think you are very skilled at measuring who people are. If they're not what they should be, it's as though your 'metal detector' goes off and warns us ahead of time not to get involved with them. I really appreciate that about you."

Object:_____
Why did you choose it?

c. Positive symbols

For example, if your wife is very positive—even early in the morning—you could say, "Diane, from the moment you get up, it's like watching the traffic light turn green. It's full speed ahead, and you're ready to get moving."

Positive symbol:_____
Why did you choose it?

CHAPTER EIGHT

LEAVING HOME

KEY THOUGHT

In order to cleave to your mate you must truly leave your parents, your past, and other prior attachments. A healthy relationship with parents means a breaking of emotional dependence.

1. Go back to the general time period when you left home permanently. What part of the "letting go" process was smooth and healthy? What part may have been unpleasant and hurtful? Why?

2. What words, responses, and actions toward your mate may still be conditioned by a relationship to your parents? Which ones are helpful and which are harmful?

3. Like Solomon, you may be attempting to get your mate to move on in the journey, away from "disquieting thoughts" from the past. What can you do to encourage your mate regarding past problems with parental (or other) relationships?

4. Sins can be generational; the tendencies and effects can be handed down unwittingly. Examine the weaknesses of your parents. Are they being duplicated, even in a subtle way, as you relate to your spouse? Pray for forgiveness, healing, and the willingness to take the necessary steps to break the cycle.

5. Discuss what your parents did right in rearing you. Even if you didn't come from a completely wonderful home, you have benefited from positives that should be reinforced in your relationship with your spouse.

CHAPTER NINE

WALKING TOWARD CLOSENESS

KEY THOUGHT

Relationships level out when children leave their parents. This equality implies healthy boundaries, allowing Christ to meet needs where our parents failed, and, at times, attempting reconciliation.

1. Even if your family ghosts have been discussed in relation to chapter 8, make sure you have received all the necessary insight, forgiveness, and reconciliation needed, so as not to put obstacles in the way of your spouse.

2. When you think of separation from your parents, is there a particular event that has symbolic significance to you? Why and how did it contribute to a horizontal relationship?

3. What particular boundaries were (and are) necessary to maintain a healthy relationship with your parents? How should diplomacy, tact, or even word picture comparisons be used in your case to keep these boundaries intact?

4. If you feel it is necessary, helpful, and appropriate, go to one or both of your parents and attempt to deal with unresolved conflicts, unmet needs, etc. Do not be judgmental, controlling, or have your own agenda. Seek forgiveness, restoration, and healing.

5. We often concentrate on the negative when analyzing how we act (or react) in a similar fashion to our parents. Make a list of all the positive traits, attitudes, and behaviors inherited from your parents. Share the list with them, if possible. Then seek ways to increase this legacy in relation to your spouse.

CHAPTER TEN

CHASING THE PREDATORS

KEY THOUGHT

Small, neglected, or even unnoticed "little things" that are negative can turn into large problems, if not recognized and dealt with promptly. Daily maintenance of the details in your relationship prevents deterioration.

1. The author mentions a few of the "little foxes" that will cause damage if repeated, such as telling only part of the truth to "protect" your spouse and bouncing a check. Make a list of your own actions that might fall into this category, based on the last year of personal behavior. How can you make sure you won't repeat them?

2. Listening to your spouse's warning regarding small issues can save you in areas such as time, money, and relational stress. Think back and acknowledge what you saved in both negative and positive ways by heeding your mate's counsel.

3. Carefully examine each item on the following list to determine whether you've contributed to "little foxes" becoming "lions." Work with your mate on a plan for change.

4. With your husband or wife contract a plan that will help to put problems in perspective, creating concrete steps for change (in the following ways):

a) Unresolved emotional earthquakes

a) Avoid tactics that repeatedly don't work

b) Physical distance in communication

b) Celebrate your strengths/successes

c) Interruptions and lack of listening

c) Clearly define a workable goal

d) Avoiding difficult issues

d) Break down the goal into definable steps

e) Offensive tone of voice

e) Reward each other for progress

f) Words that wound

f) Remain open to changes at various stages of life

g) Nonverbal abuse

CHAPTER ELEVEN

ENJOYING PHYSICAL INTIMACY

KEY THOUGHT

Many important ingredients are necessary to attain a fulfilling sexual relationship. In addition to avoiding stimulation or temptations outside of marriage, you need to focus on your various needs, backgrounds, communication, and spirituality to experience strong sexual intimacy.

1. Our society spreads much misinformation about sex. Apart from obvious immorality, give examples from various media that are more subtle: "super sex," national norms, etc. How might these and other partial myths negatively affect your own special, unique relationship?

2. Strong boundaries involving marital faithfulness are necessary for continuing intimacy. Be honest about the types of reading or viewing media—or inappropriate contact with members of the opposite sex—that can or have caused you to cross the line mentally, verbally, or physically. Seek forgiveness and ways to avoid a recurrence.

3. Rate yourself on a scale from one to ten in the following areas that affect your sexual response to your spouse. With 1=very negative and 10=very positive (5 is neutral), where do you rate on each of these "Layers of Life"?

_____ Physical differences (persona and gender)

_____ Personal past sexual experience

_____ Family history (experience and attitudes)

_____ Present environmental factors

_____ Influence of cultural values

_____ Present physical and level of the spiritual
commitment emotional needs

4. Though, as adults, we feel we should know everything
about sex, we are ignorant in numerous areas: physiology,
emotions, and even spiritual aspects of our sexuality.
Make a choice to read one of the books on sexual intimacy suggested by the author, or at least some other Chris-
tian-based book or article that will teach you more about
this subject.

CHAPTER TWELVE

ʟEADERSHIP THAT DRAWS ʈWO TOGETHER

Key Thought

The goal of godly leadership is to create a two-part harmony where both partners complement each other as they glide in the same direction. This begins with male leadership that is based on both Solomon and Christ: loving, guiding, serving, and caring.

1. True leadership by a man draws the woman by love, service, and sound judgment. Yet poor models of past male leadership affect both the man and the woman in the relationship. Take a joint look at your pasts to determine why and how your negative reactions impede the flow of healthy leadership.

2. Now make a list of positive leadership traits acted out in your families. How have they influenced the effectiveness of your own qualities in this regard? How can the further emphasis on these attributes help minimize the negatives you discussed in question 1?

3. Take a good look at all the various sides of anger in your relationship: repressed/out-of-control, righteous/unrighteous, etc. What are the root causes of unhealthy expressions of anger, and how does such anger hamper godly leadership? Seek forgiveness and reconciliation regarding the bad fruit of unrighteous anger from the past. Devise three steps to create healthy boundaries.

4. All of us fear some sort of failure in such a challenging task as leading and responding in a relationship. Make a list of every fear you have, based on past performance, present concerns, or future challenges. Then construct a second column and title it "opportunities," linking each fear to what can become an accomplishment.

5. Though the man takes the lead in drawing the woman onward in God's plan, it's important that both have a vision for the future. Share your plans, hopes, and dreams with each other, being careful to include the spiritual element as central to your future happiness together.

CHAPTER 13

BUILDING YOUR LIFE ACCORDING TO CODE

KEY THOUGHT

The only sure foundation for an intimate relationship is the Lord Jesus Christ. As with any worthwhile building, a solid foundation and strong materials are essential. Building upon Christ includes Bible study, prayer, worship, and accountability.

1. You may praise your mate for his or her beauty, but do you appreciate the benefits of the spiritual fruit in his or her life? Write a letter to your mate, expressing appreciation for the benefits you've received from your partner's spiritual growth and faithfulness to Christ.

2. Use your own word picture to describe the kind of "house" you would like to build in your relationship, based on Christ as a foundation. What would the various materials and ornaments represent in terms of attitudes, actions, events, etc., that further the intimacy factor?

3. Rate yourself from A to F in each of the following areas, based on where you are right now in the spiritual disciplines. Then create a concrete plan to improve your grade.

_____ a) prayer and worship (personal and corporate)

_____ b) Bible study (personal and corporate)

_____ c) family devotions

_____ d) giving (time and money)

_____ e) other church activities (spiritual)

4. Though we have freedom to set our own personal worship times, the best quiet time is early morning. Regardless of your set time, what are the distractions that most prevent you from accomplishing your spiritual goals? Devise a plan to minimize or eliminate these interruptions in order to be more effective.

5. The point of this chapter is to show that personal spiritual growth is critical to increasing intimacy. But sharing your spiritual life with your mate is equally important. Discuss a joint strategy to pray together for each other's needs and to share the wisdom of the Scriptures. Make it either a short time together daily or a longer time once a week.

CHAPTER FOURTEEN

PLANNED SPONTANEITY

KEY THOUGHT

1. The following commitment card, signed and dated, is a good way for you and your spouse to seal an agreement to spend time together during a Personal Enrichment Weekend. Read it, sign it, and then make plans to enjoy a time of refreshment and growth together.

COUPLE COMMITMENT CARD

Because we want our relationship to honor God, be personally fulfilling, and be a loving testimony to our children and others, we're committed to going on this weekend trip together. We purpose to look at the eight pictures of love in Song of Songs and see how we can better live them out. We promise to each other and before God that during the weekend we'll do our utmost to keep our tone of voice honoring at all times, and that if we have to take a short break from a difficult subject, we'll come back together within half an hour, hold hands, and pray together before moving on. Our goal isn't to solve every problem or decide every issue. It's to focus on our marriage this one weekend—not the children or our careers—and have a warm, loving time together as we "come away to the country" to experience more of God's best.

Signed this _____ day of _____, before God and my spouse.

_____   _____
            Husband   Wife

Optional Intimacy Exercise

The following optimal intimacy exercise has sometimes been called the "non-demand" intimacy exercise, for it puts no expectation upon the response of the receiving person. In fact, it specifically requests no sexual response. It is recommended as part of your Personal Enrichment Weekend.

With the door locked and the phone off the hook, begin by taking a shower together. Then return to the bedroom with the lights down low. One person begins as the "pleasuring" partner whose goal it is to give the most luxurious head-to-toe, and front-and-back, back rub and massage possible in a fifteen-minute time frame.

This begins with the first "pleasuring" partner having his or her spouse lie face down on the bed, and then starting with a scalp massage, moving down the neck and back all the way to the toes (which some people enjoy having massaged, while others scream if they're even touched!). That's a key point of this exercise—to see what type of touching and what "likes and dislikes" your spouse has.

Once the "pleasuring" partner has gone head to toe, finding out what the spouse likes, gently ask him or her to turn over and start again at the head and move down to the toes. However, *there should be no genital touching during this exercise.* The goal here isn't intercourse, but pleasuring the other person. That takes the pressure off of "having to make love" and onto learning how to relax and enjoy each other's physical presence apart from sex.

When you've gone head to toe, both front and back, and your fifteen minutes are up, then switch places. Now the spouse who has been massaged becomes the "pleasuring" partner, and he or she goes through the exercise for fifteen minutes.

When both people have finished their fifteen minutes, then simply hold each other, *again without any expectation or demand for intercourse at this time.* That's important to agree on *before* doing this exercise or the potential for spoiling a very special experience is almost assured. It's a myth that men or women will "explode" if they get excited and don't come to "fulfillment" right then. *If you agree to do this exercise, then you're agreeing to cuddle and kiss for the next half hour if you'd like, but do not engage in intercourse until after that time.*

Moody Press, a ministry of Moody Bible Institute,
is designed for education, evangelization, and edification.
If we may assist you in knowing more about Christ
and the Christian life, please write us without obligation:
Moody Press, c/o MLM, Chicago, Illinois 60610.